PINES

MW01716825

Contents

First published in the United States of America in 2005 by
Stone Lantern Publishing
A division of Stone Lantern Discoveries, Inc.
125 Meeting House Hill
Passumpsic, VT 05861

Copyright 2005 by Stone Lantern Publishing

Edited and adapted by Wayne Schoech and Michael Persiano.

Design by Joseph Schoech.

Some text and photos are originally from Kindai Bonsai and
Bonsai Today magazines.

All rights reserved. No part of this publication may be reproduced
in any manner whatsoever without permission in writing from
Stone Lantern Publishing.

ISBN: 0-9767550-0-9
LC 2005903091

Printed and bound in the U.S.A.

Preface

The idea for a series of books based on articles from out-of-print issues of ***Bonsai Today*** had been kicking around for awhile when I mentioned it to Michael Persiano during a phone conversation about an article Michael was writing.

I felt a book on Japanese pines was the right place to start, and Michael was quite enthusiastic. He offered to help by selecting suitable chapters from out-of-print issues of Bonsai Today, and filling in with general sections on care and other important topics. At the time I was in over my head trying to figure out how to be an editor and publisher of Bonsai Today, so I gladly accepted.

Almost immediately my inbox began filling up with chapters. A lot of them were still quite rough*, but we were underway. The book you are now holding had begun to take shape.

Now, more than two years later, it's finally finished. Though we had some great material to start with, much has been rewritten and much has been added. The more we dug in, the more we changed and elaborated. For me, it became an obsession. The more I did, the more I noticed had to be done. And so it went.

Finally, after countless rewrites and edits, and equally countless proofings, I decided it was finished. Though more improvements could always be made, it's time to make our offering and let you be the judge. I sincerely hope you find it worth the wait.

My heartfelt thanks to Michael Persiano whose push-start and on-going efforts were invaluable; to Mary Lang who struggled mightily with messy manuscripts and never lost her sense of humor; to Leonora Foslund, whose tireless proofing and intelligent comments helped push this book up the final incline; to Vanna Guldenschuh who fearlessly took over the daily operations of Stone Lantern in order to free me up, and then graciously reminded me whenever I strayed very far from this book; to John Palmer, founder of Bonsai Today — without John, there wouldn't be a Bonsai Today or a pine book; and to my son, Joseph Schoech, the designer of this book and Bonsai Today, for being a friend, consultant and confidant every step of the way.

Yours in beautiful and healthy bonsai,
Wayne Schoech
Editor and Publisher
Stone Lantern Publishing and Bonsai Today magazine

**If you go back to the original articles that most of the chapters are drawn from, you'll notice that little remains exactly as it was. Most of the early translations were quite rough, and the people doing the early edits were still learning the subtleties of bonsai. In addition to re-editing and elaborating, we've added commentaries in italics. These are designed to fill in where holes exist. Most were written with newer enthusiasts in mind, as much is assumed in the originals. I hope you find them useful.*

Introduction

Nature has presented us with the fascinating juxtaposition of the Japanese white and black pines. No two species better represent classical bonsai art. *Pinus parviflora* (Japanese white pine) prefers cooler climates and expresses the delicate grace of nature, while *Pinus thunbergii* (Japanese black pine) prefers warmer climates and expresses the raw power of nature. While these species often challenge the bonsai artist, both promise great rewards when approached with respect for their essential natures.

Several factors are critical to the development of pine bonsai, but nothing is more important than the mastery of technique. ***Bonsai Today's Pines*** presents informative and insightful projects by some of the finest bonsai masters in the world, including: Oishi Kasan, Masahiko Kimura, Mikio Oshima, Mitsuya Sose, Tomio Yamada, Takeshita Yosiaki, and others. Also included are two general primers on Japanese white and black pine development.

Because this book has been written for intermediate and advanced bonsai enthusiasts (as well as daring beginners), the most basic aspects of bonsai culture are only briefly discussed. Beginners seeking additional information on general styling, wiring, potting, and other basics of the art, can choose from a number of excellent books offered by *Stone Lantern Publishing*, the publishers of this book and *Bonsai Today* magazine.

This book is organized into two sections: Japanese white pines and Japanese black pines. Each section begins with a chapter on care and maintenance and is followed by a series of projects, logically sequenced and prefaced by introductory notes. Within each chapter, italicized entries expand on the author's content, offer insight into Japanese terminology, and provide supplemental information on related techniques. The profusion of color photographs in each chapter show the dramatic changes resulting from the winning combination of technical mastery and artistic inspiration.

Wayne Schoech and I, as well as others associated with *Bonsai Today* and *Stone Lantern Publishing*, have worked hard to make ***Pines*** a valuable and timeless reference that you can return to year after year. While this book presents a variety of approaches for styling and developing Japanese white and black pines, the quest to express natural beauty through bonsai emerges as a common theme throughout.

We wish you great success and sincerely hope that this book will add to your enjoyment and mastery of the art of bonsai

Michael Persiano

WHITE PINES

INTRODUCTION TO THE WORLD OF

Japanese White Pines

by Michael Persiano with Wayne Schoech

A good example of just how elegantly beautiful a Japanese white pine can be. Bunjin (literati) style . Height 39" (99 cm). From Japan, artist unknown.

OVERVIEW

The Japanese white pine's versatility, natural beauty and grace, make it a favorite of bonsai enthusiasts throughout the world.

Before we focus on bonsai, it may be worthwhile to visit ***Yogo***, the 600-year-old white pine at the temple of *Zen-Yioji* in Tokyo prefecture. Yogo is one of the most interesting trees anywhere, and has no doubt inspired countless people to try their hands at growing white pines, either in their gardens or as bonsai. Yogo's canopy measures 98′ (30 m) from east to west and 92′ (28 m) from north to south. Its trunk diameter is 12′ (3.7 m), while its height is only 23′ (7 m).

The Japanese white pine (*Pinus parviflora*), is one of only nine five-needle pines in the world – if you live in the eastern U.S., you are no doubt familiar with the Eastern white pine (*Pinus strobus*).

There are more than 150 known cultivars of the Japanese white pine. The photographs on the next page show some of the cultivars used for bonsai. The average length, color, and texture of needles can vary significantly from cultivar to cultivar. Care and shaping techniques may also vary.

Yogo, at the entry to *Zen-Yioji*. It's hard to believe that this canopy belongs to one tree.

The poles are an ingenious way to expand the canopy.

NEEDLES OF JAPANESE WHITE PINE VARIETIES

Aoi

Azuma-tendiu

Zuisho

Kokonoe

Hoku-azuma

Azuma-tendai

Azuma-nishiki

Horai

Haniri-yanomi

Hinirishi

Haniryoko

Orizurui-ba

GENERAL INFORMATION

Needles

All white pine needles grow in bundles (clusters) of five. Japanese white pine needles are semi-rigid and stay on the tree for 2-3 years in tufts at branch tips. They are 1" - 2" (5 cm) in length and can be reduced to about 1" (2.5 cm) in bonsai culture.

Bark

Immature trees show light gray bark, while mature trees develop a darker gray. Trees grafted onto Japanese black pine trunks rapidly develop fissured bark. Non-grafted white pines slowly develop scaly bark. *The fissured bark referred to is actually the bark on the black pine stock. Grafts typically are 6" or higher up the black pine trunk. The scaly bark characteristic of white pines develops on the wood above the graft.*

Growth habit

Goyomatsu foliage is generally quite dense. In nature, young trees have pyramidal shapes, while older trees develop flat tops. The tree's natural growth patterns easily conform to most bonsai styles.

Size

In nature, Japanese white pines can reach 50'-70' (15-21 m). In bonsai culture, most range from 1-3.' Taller specimens (up to 4') occasionally occur, especially in literati style.

Hardiness

Zones 4 to 7. In-ground trees can survive temperatures down to -24 degrees Fahrenheit (-31 Celsius). Winter dormancy is critical to long-term health. See pages 18 & 19 or consult your local bonsai nursery or club to determine the best approach to wintering in your area.

Growth rate

In nature, Japanese white pines grow at a moderate rate. In bonsai pots, their growth rate depends upon a number of factors. Accelerated growth and increased density can be achieved through aggressive feeding and energy balancing.

Sunlight

Full sun is essential to ensure health.

Diseases

Needle cast, rust, root-rot, dieback, tip blight and canker are some common diseases found on Japanese white pines.

Insects

Some insects that are fond of *goyomatsu* are: sawflies, pine webworm, scale, needle miner, white pine aphids, bark beetles and shoot borers.

CARE & MAINTENANCE

Soil

To optimize root growth and minimize root-rot, use a fast-draining soil. Rather than debate the merits of countless soils (*there are almost as many soil mixes as there are enthusiasts*), we would like to suggest two that many growers have used with success.

Needles of *Pinus parviflora* growing in nature.

***Goyomatsu* bark**

Akadama

Akadama

Literally translated, akadama means red clay balls. Akadama is the standard soil for most conifers, including pines. It is excavated from quarries (between an upper layer of topsoil and a lower level of sand) in *Akagi-yama* in Honshu, 75 miles north of Tokyo. The excavated akadama is not fired, but dried in hothouses, as firing substantially increases akadama's water retention capacity, and can contribute to root-rot.

Akadama has a pH of 6.5 to 6.9, slightly acidic to neutral. Many enthusiasts use 100% akadama, particularly for pines and other conifers. You can also use akadama as an ingredient in your current soil mix, as it works well in combination with other soil components.

Akadama drains extremely well, retaining only optimal amounts of water. This encourages maximum root vitality and discourages root-rot. Although akadama comes neatly packaged, it is important to screen out most of the fine powder (you'll never get it all out) to ensure optimal water penetration. The powder can be used later as a component in muck for root-over-rock or slab plantings.

Akadama has a low cation exchange capacity, meaning it does not hold nutrients as well as some soils. Because ongoing access to essential nutrients is so important, it is a good idea to use slow-release fertilizers with akadama.

Akadama comes in soft, medium and hard granules. Most people use soft granules, though if you live in a wet climate, you might try medium granules. Very few people use the hardest granules by themselves. If you use the hardest granules, try them in combination with soft or medium granules (or other ingredients) at a ratio of no more than 50%.

Akadama granules also come in various sizes. Generally, the larger the tree and pot, the larger the granules should be.

In general, akadama is the standard soil for pines, and countless bonsai enthusiasts and professionals have experienced outstanding results using it. However, because akadama is imported from Japan, cost can become an issue, especially if you have a large conifer collection.

A domestic mix

Turface, bark, haydite, coarse sand and a small amount of mycorrhizal fungi medium is a fairly common mix used by American bonsai enthusiasts and professionals. It consists of equal parts of each of the four main components and about one tablespoon of mycorrhizal fungi medium per gallon of soil. These components can usually be purchased reasonably at nurseries or agricultural outlets. After thoroughly mixing the ingredients, screen out the finest particles (fines) to ensure optimal water penetration and drainage. Double or even triple screening is good.

Mychorrhizal fungi

The following is from ***planthealthcare.com***: *"To survive, most plant species established a symbiotic partnership with a unique group of soil organisms called mycorrhizal fungi. These fungi are considered by plant scientists to be the biological cornerstone of plant life on earth. This little-known family of beneficial fungi live in and around the roots of 95% of the earth's plant species, serving as a secondary root system that extends far out into the soil. Mycorrhizae extract mineral elements and water from soil for their host plant, and live off the plant's sugars. Trees and plants with thriving mycorrhizal roots are better able to survive and thrive in stressful man-made environments."*

Pines are quite dependent on mycorrhizal fungi, and it is a good idea to add it whenever you transplant. Be sure to mix it directly into the soil. It doesn't work if you simply sprinkle it on the surface.

Commercial and other mixes

Commercial bonsai mixes are often (though not always) quite good and are readily purchased through bonsai nurseries and suppliers. You can also experiment with any number of mixes of your own creation. Consult your local bonsai club to determine what mixes enthusiasts in your area are using.

POTTING

The best time to pot Japanese white pines is in the spring, just before the buds begin to swell. Although late summer or early fall potting is an option, it is best to avoid heavy rootpruning just before winter, unless you live in a mild climate. Potting procedures for white pines are much the same as for other pines. See pages 130-139 for details.

AFTERCARE

Shade

Freshly repotted trees are more vulnerable to stress than established trees, especially if they have been heavily rootpruned. It is best to keep your trees out of the hot afternoon sun for two to three weeks after potting. Light shade with early morning sun is best.

Watering

The margin of error is less with freshly potted trees than with established trees. Be careful. Don't let the soil become bone-dry and conversely, don't let the soil stay soggy. Soggy soil is a very real risk, since a freshly potted tree will use less water than a vigorous established tree.

Rooting stimulant

For the first month or so, apply a root stimulant every second or third time you water to help mitigate transplant shock and accelerate root growth.

WIRING

Japanese white pines can be wired almost any time of year. Our preference is to wire during the growing season (early spring to early fall). While it is not unusual for wire to be left on a pine for a year (or even longer), it is good to periodically check to make sure the wire is not cutting into the bark. If the wire is starting to cut, it is time to remove it. Though you can unravel the wire in order to reuse it, it is easier and safer to cut it off in small sections. If you forget (or neglect) to take the wire off in time, don't be too alarmed if it has cut into the bark. Though it is best to avoid wire scars, you are not likely to encounter a Japanese white pine that will not outgrow unsightly scars in two to three years.

You can use either copper or aluminum wire on white pines. Stiff annealed solid copper wire is best for major bending, to optimize holding power. More forgiving aluminum wire is good for finer bending and in situations where you are likely to make numerous adjustments.

ENERGY BALANCING

A prerequisite to successfully growing Japanese white pines is understanding energy balancing techniques. Candle pinching, shoot pruning, needle plucking and bud removal are the keys to developing well-balanced horizontal growth and impressive overall designs.The following approach is simple and easily executed. *Because energy balancing is essential for shaping white pines (and other pines), it is covered several times in this book. Though each approach is a little different, they all end up in the same place – with well-balanced vigorous white pines.*

Pinching candles in the spring

Before pinching back new candles, study your tree and identify the strong, medium, and weak growth zones.

Strong zones are usually on or near the top of the tree and weak zones are usually lower. This is because pines (and most other trees) tend to be apically dominant (they put most of their energy into the top of the tree).

Sunlight is the other determining factor in creating strong and weak zones. Identification of the zones is easy, as the strong zones are full of vigorous lush foliage, and the weak zones are not.

Once you have identified the zones, and the buds have elongated into tight cylindric candles, use your thumb and index finger to pinch off up to 75% of the candles in the strongest zones. About 10 days later, pinch off 50-75% of the strongest candles in the medium zones. Don't pinch candles in the weak zones.

If pinching is done properly, you will redirect energy from the strongest zones to the medium and weak zones, balancing the overall growth of the tree. Though properly pinching candles is best, if you are uncomfortable doing this, you can allow them to develop into shoots (just wait until they open and extend) and prune them back based on the following information.

Shoot pruning - spring & summer

You need to prune your Japanese white pine for overall design and to promote budding. *Even if you have pinched off candles, the remaining ones will become shoots, which will need pruning.* Unlike Japanese black and red pines, Japanese white pines are less forgiving when over-pruned. Hard cuts that totally eliminate a season's new growth can kill a branch. It is critical that you leave 4-5 bundles of new needles on each shoot when you prune the strong and medium zones. Do not prune in the weak zone.

Needle plucking — summer & fall

Removing old needles allows light and air to get to the inside of the tree and helps redirect energy to the new shoots. Old needle clusters (or bundles) can be distinguished from new needle clusters by their location (further from the tips of the branches) and their faded, aged appearance. Pluck very carefully without tearing the bark. If, after plucking the old needles in a strong zone, the branch is still too heavy with foliage, you can remove some of the newer needles. Leave at least 4-5 clusters on each shoot. If too many new needles are removed before next year's buds form, the branch is likely to die.

Sometimes needle plucking results in excessive bleeding. Experiment on an expendable shoot to determine how much needle plucking your tree can tolerate. If you notice excessive sap flow after plucking a few needles, try trimming the old needles instead of plucking. Use sharp clean shears and carefully cut each cluster, leaving approximately 1/16." The stubs will fall off later.

Bud removal

The last step in energy balancing is removing unwanted buds. This should be done when you finish needle plucking. Remove buds that are growing very close together and strong buds (the largest ones) in strong zones. Be careful to leave at least four or five buds on each shoot.

Most people use their fingers to remove unwanted buds. If your fingers are too large, or you have difficulty isolating buds, use tweezers. If you prefer using other tools designed for this task, consider purchasing bud shears or very narrow concave cutters that are designed for bud removal. No matter what you use, be careful not to damage other nearby buds.

WATERING & POSITIONING

Success with bonsai hinges on understanding the relationship between watering and positioning. Each and every bonsai has unique watering needs and the location you choose will affect those needs.

One way to determine when your tree needs water is to insert a chopstick into the root pad, and check it daily. Pull the chopstick out and touch the portion that has been in the soil. When the chopstick is on the dry side, it is time to water thoroughly. Don't forget to check regularly. Drying out too much can be deadly.

Where you place your tree will affect how frequently you water. During the growing season (early spring to early/mid-fall), place your pine in direct sunlight for optimal results. If you live in a relatively cool and damp climate, you may need to water only every other day (even less in some cases). Conversely, if you live in a hot, dry climate, you may need to water once or even twice a day.

Most problems with bonsai arise from drying out due to neglect, too frequent watering, poor choice of growing location, or some combination of these conditions. If you want healthy trees, you must master the art of watering, pay attention to proper positioning, and follow a few other simple guidelines. *It is important to understand that watering needs will change as the weather changes. Though this may seem obvious, it is always surprising how many people think they can put their bonsai on a regular watering schedule. What you should put on a regular schedule is checking the soil for moisture.*

If your tree becomes stressed, you will most likely find that the soil is staying wet for days and only needs to be watered occasionally. No matter what the cause of the original stress, excessively wet soil means root-rot. If your tree is suffering from root-rot, you must cut off all the rotten (dark or even black) roots, soak the remaining roots in a fungicide (someone at a local nursery should be able to suggest something suitable) for fifteen minutes, then repot in a scrubbed pot with fresh soil. Otherwise severe damage or even death can result.

FERTILIZING

All plants require nitrogen, phosphoric acid, and potassium (N-P-K), as well as trace minerals and other nutrients. If your pine is young, liberally apply fertilizers, or even use Superfeeding (see page 36), to encourage vigorous healthy growth. *Many beginners (and others) underfeed their trees and then wonder why they perform poorly. Feed regularly and generously during the growing season and you'll be amazed at the results. To avoid root burn, try organic slow-release fertilizers. If you use strong liquid fertilizers, frequent diluted applications are better than occasional full-strength doses.*

Feeding should begin in the early spring and continue until late summer. Though there are numerous perfectly good feeding programs you can use, here are three that we like:

Cakes

Fertilizer cakes are an excellent slow-release fertilizer. Recipes range from rapeseed as a base to more complex mixtures. The following recipe is one we recommend based upon our experience.

3 parts cottonseed meal - 2 parts garden lime - 1 part blood meal (nitrogen and iron) - 1 part bone meal (phosphorus) - commercial solution of full-strength 20-30-20 diluted with water - fish emulsion (five ounces for every five pounds of dry ingredients).

After dry mixing the first four ingredients, add all the liquids until the mixture is the consistency of cooked oatmeal. Spread the fertilizer in a flat tray. Score the fertilizer into squares about 1.5" (4 cm) across with a moistened paint stirrer, and set the rack in the sun to dry. Once the cakes have completely dried, snap into squares and place in a sealed container for future use.

During the growing season place enough cakes on top of the soil to cover about 20% of the soil surface. Some people use even more, as the cakes break down slowly and the risk of over-feeding is low (provided the soil drains well).

If you use cakes, rake the surface of the soil once a month to ensure adequate water penetration. Because heavy fertilizing results in rapid root growth, you'll need to repot every one to two years.

Liquid fertilizers

Any balanced fertilizer will satisfy the needs of your Japanese white pine, though it is a good idea to alternate at least two types to insure a broader spectrum of nutrients. Prepare the mixtures according to the manufacturer's instructions. *If you are using a strong fertilizer on a mildly stressed tree (severely stressed trees should not be fertilized at all until they start to recover), dilute to about 1/3 strength for the first few feedings. Once the tree has perked up, you can use a stronger solution. Some people are wary of using strong chemical fertilizers at full strength, even with robust trees. If you are the cautious type, you can always dilute to half strength.*

Superfeeding

Superfeeding is an aggressive feeding program developed by Michael Persiano. See page 36 for a complete description.

WINTER STORAGE

Japanese white pines require a dormant period to stay healthy. Undoubtedly, someone somewhere has succeeded in keeping one alive without a real period of cold dormancy, but for optimal health they should be grown where temperatures remain near, or below freezing, for at least eight weeks in mid-winter.

Some popular methods used for wintering Japanese white pines include cold frames (including poly-bench coldframes), sheds, and garages. Whatever method you select, it is critical that you provide enough air circulation to prevent fungus and deter insects from nesting.

We have experimented successfully with two storage methods: benches covered with poly sheeting and cold sheds. Details for each follows.

Benches with poly sheeting

These are simply display benches that are covered with co-poly plastic. Cover the area under the benches with cedar mulch, and position your bonsai on the mulch. Cover the pots with landscape fabric and then bury the pot and the base of the trunk up to the first branch, with cedar mulch. Insert a chopstick through the mulch and fabric to monitor the tree's water needs during the winter. The layer of mulch minimizes freeze-thaw cycles and prevents root damage.

Unless you live in a mild climate, use fairly thick plastic (8-12 mil). Staple it into place on both sides and also secure it on the bottom back of the bench. On days when temperatures are well above freezing and not too windy, pull up the plastic on the front of the bench. In the evening, lower the plastic back over the front of the bench and secure it with elastic cords connected to u-shaped nails.

Michael A. Dirr's ***Manual of Woody Landscape Plants***, asserts that in-ground Japanese white pines can take temperatures down to -24 degrees Fahrenheit (-31 Celsius), but it is unlikely that a potted Japanese white pine could survive such extreme cold for long. Our poly-bench coldframe has successfully protected Japanese white pines in night-time temperatures as low as -2 degrees Fahrenheit (-19 Celsius), with several weeks of daytime temperatures in the low teens and single digits Fahrenheit.

Sheds and other outbuildings

If you live in a climate with night-time temperatures down to about 0 degrees Fahrenheit (-17 Celsius), any well-insulated garage or outbuilding should provide adequate protection. If you live in a colder climate, or if your outbuilding is not insulated, you might want to follow these instructions: Dump a few inches of cedar mulch on top of styrofoam sheeting. Then position your bonsai and place landscape fabric and mulch as previously described under *poly-bench coldframes*.

Good ventilation is very important, no matter what system you use. If you use an outbuilding, you can position an oscillating fan near a slightly open window (but not too close to your trees) and run it during the day. Be sure to close the window at night. When day temperatures climb several degrees above freezing, open the shed doors and windows by day and close them at night.

A cold weather fluorescent light can be installed for night-time inspection of your trees. The light is not for your trees – below 36 degrees (2 degrees Celsius) or so, trees do not photosynthesize and do not need light.

In-ground cold frames

Another wintering option is a deep cold frame. These can work in extreme cold if they are built properly. Though we are not going to provide building instructions, here are a few helpful tips: build your cold frame in the shade and in a well-drained area where flooding is unlikely. Dig a foot or two below the frostline and lay in a bed of pebbles at least 8" (20 cm) deep on the bottom. Build a well-sealed wooden box above the hole with a trap door that can be opened on warm days.

Low intensity heat

Another option for very cold climates is an outbuilding with one of the following: electric gro-mats, small heaters, lights that give off heat, or other types of low-intensity heat. Make sure whatever heat source you use is far enough away from your trees to prevent hot spots, and close enough to prevent cold damage.

Some people winter their bonsai in attached garages or basement bulkheads. No matter what option you use, make sure temperatures stay below 40 Fahrenheit (4 Celsius) in order to keep your trees dormant.

Michael's poly-bench coldframe. On warm days, he opens it to let a little air in.

It's important to seal it tightly to keep cold air out.

Bunji cords and rocks are used for extra stability against wind and other forces.

The following chapters provide an abundance of information on Japanese white pine styling, care, and maintenance from some of the most notable bonsai artists in the world. While their methods vary, their work ultimately achieves the same goal: outstanding trees.

Masahiko Kimura

TRANSFORMS A SEMI-CASCADE

Masahiko Kimura is one of the greatest living bonsai masters. His work with pines is legendary in Japan and the west. In this chapter, Mr. Kimura elevates a medium-sized, unstyled semi-cascade into a specimen whose beauty emerges with the development of a clearly defined crown and three additional foliage pads. Key techniques demonstrated in this section include: the aging of bark, needle plucking, candle pinching, pruning, and shaping with wire.

The pine as originally acquired by Mr. Kimura in the spring of 1985.
Pinus parviflora. Height 16" (41 cm). width 19" (48 cm).

Mr. Kimura intended to cut back the longest branch. But he decides to wait and this proves fortuitous; later he decides the extra length can be used to extend and accentuate the cascading effect.

Left view.

Back view.

BALANCING GROWTH

Mr. Kimura purchased this fifteen year-old, field-grown *Pinus parviflora var. Azuma* for about twenty dollars. This project reveals a rarely seen side of Kimura; rather than a magician who mysteriously transforms unlikely specimens into beautiful trees in a few hours, here he is a patient grower and artist who knows how to improve the health and general development of a tree before working his magic.

Because this specimen has been neglected, the first task is simply to provide good general care. Once health and vitality are restored, shaping can begin. *This is a theme that appears over and over again with the best bonsai artists. Be patient. Bring your trees to peak health before you tackle them in earnest. Aside from the obvious advantage of having trees that are better able to withstand and recover from restyling, you have a chance to get to know your trees and contemplate their potential before you start restyling.*

Although the foliage was wild and gangly when Mr. Kimura acquired the tree, it's still good quality bonsai material. The line of the trunk is quite suitable for semi-cascade style. Unfortunately, the roots and trunk show the signs of a young tree forced to grow too quickly in the seller's nursery.

Before starting, Mr. Kimura decides to age the bark on the lower trunk and exposed roots by placing the tree close to a wall, with the trunk in shade and the foliage in direct sunlight. In nature, the north faces of trees become covered with moss and cracks, aging long before the sides which receive more sun. You can see from the picture that this simple technique achieves the desired effect.

Shaping a Japanese white pine consists mostly of pinching back candles, pruning shoots and plucking needles and buds. Pinching candles in the spring slows the growth of the strongest shoots during the tree's most vigorous growing stage. This makes it much easier to keep the tree in scale. *This also redirects energy to other parts of the tree. For detailed instruction on pinching candles, see the next chapter.*

Pruning shoots corrects the length of the youngest branches. This is done at the beginning of summer and stimulates back buds and shoots, increasing density and forcing horizontal growth. *For more detailed instruction on pruning shoots, see the next chapter.*

Plucking needles and buds is a task for the fall. First remove all the three-year-old needles and reduce the number of newer needles in the areas of strong growth. *Be careful to leave at least four to five bundles (needle clusters) on each shoot. If too many needles are removed before the new buds are formed, the shoot or branch could easily die.* Three-year-old needles are found on the inside of the branches, nearest the trunk. They're easy to identify because they will have begun to turn yellow or will have only two or three needles in each cluster instead of the usual five. *This is because some will have fallen off by now. Needle clusters on all white pines start with five needles, which is why white pines are sometimes called five-needle-pines.*

The first stage is completed. You can see how well the bark has aged. September 1989. Height 9" (23 cm). Width 22" (56 cm).

It's important not to remove any live needles from the weakest areas. Pinching candles, pruning, and plucking active needles in the strongest zones sends energy to the weak areas, eventually creating more balanced growth. These procedures need to be performed every year during the entire life of the tree. Working with Japanese white pines requires a real commitment of time and energy, but the rewards are well worth the effort.

Balancing the flow of energy in a Japanese white pine is critical to achieving your design objectives. While Mr. Kimura recommends removing two needles from a bundle of five, this approach is time-consuming and optional when dealing with healthy, vigorous trees. If you don't have the time (or patience), we recommend you do what most people do, which is to simply remove entire needle clusters.

On most varieties of Japanese white pine, the needles are not pulled off, but cut with scissors. This is to prevent tearing of the bark and excessive sap flow (*bleeding*). However, the Azuma variety from northern Japan is very strong, and needles may be pulled out by hand without damaging the bark.

Selecting and removing buds follows immediately after needle plucking. Essentially, it consists of identifying those buds that are either growing very close together or that are very strong and are in a zone that is also strong, and then removing them. In addition to removing buds, pull off some new needles in the strongest areas to balance the strong and weak areas.

Most people use their fingers to remove unwanted buds. If your fingers are too large, or you have difficulty isolating the bud, use tweezers. If you prefer using tools designed for this task, consider purchasing bud shears or very narrow concave cutters that are designed for bud removal. No matter what you use, be careful not to damage other nearby buds.

As you can see, with a few simple techniques, a good eye and some patience, Mr. Kimura succeeds in completely transforming a neglected pine into a wonderful specimen.

Before. The cascade branch from straight on (right view). Note the density of the foliage.

Bark develops rugged aged character on the north side first. This principle was used quite ingeniously by Mr. Kimura.

The three-year-old needles are nearest to the base of each branch.

To prevent bleeding, Mr. Kimura suggests you use scissors on most white pine varieties to remove old needles. Leave a small 1/16" (15 mm) stump.

When removing needles: A. In strong zones leave two or three needles per cluster. *Most people simply remove whole clusters, rather than removing individual needles, which can be quite tedious and time consuming. However, Mr. Kimura is a renowned bonsai master, and following his suggestions can be instructive and beneficial.* B. In weak zones leave all five needles per cluster.

Strong zone. The needles need to be reduced.

After needle plucking.

Leave the one-year-old needles.

Though they are difficult to see, there are some stubs on these shoots. There are also a few new buds.

With strong skinned varieties like the Azuma, you can pull the needles off with your fingers.

By the third year the needles have turned light green to yellow and there are usually only two or three left per cluster. The rest have died and fallen off.

Mr. Kimura plucks two needles per cluster in a strong zone.

When old needles are removed, the new buds receive more light and tend to grow quite rapidly.

You barely notice that so many needles and shoots have been removed.

Mr. Kimura intent on his work.

The main branch after wiring.

Next come the secondary branches.

The entire tree is now wired.

Even the tiniest branches have been wired.

After shaping. Looking good.

Avoid leaving unsightly stubs (unless you plan to use them for jin). Remember to seal with cutpaste.

Before and after the final shaping.

Pinus parviflora. Semi-cascade, *neagari* style (exposed root style; where roots form the trunk). Height: 8.5," length 21" (26cm x 53cm). *The aerial root that grows off the right of the trunk seems unsightly and distracting. We don't know if Mr. Kimura plans to remove it later when the tree is stronger, or if he feels that it adds character and interest.*

Cultivating Balance

ENERGY BALANCING AND NEEDLE REDUCTION

Artist: Takeshita Yosiaki

PINCHING CANDLES

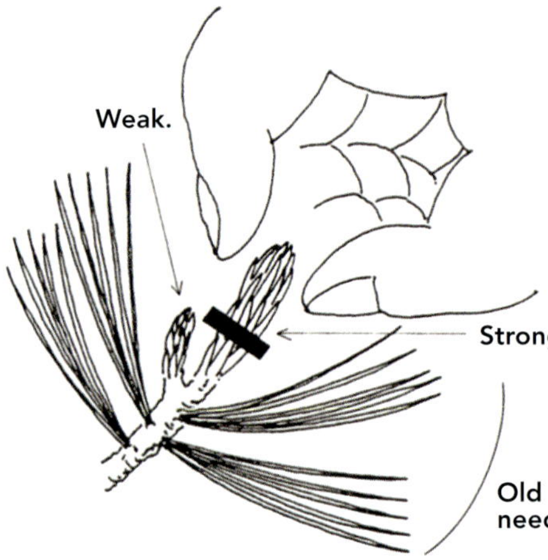

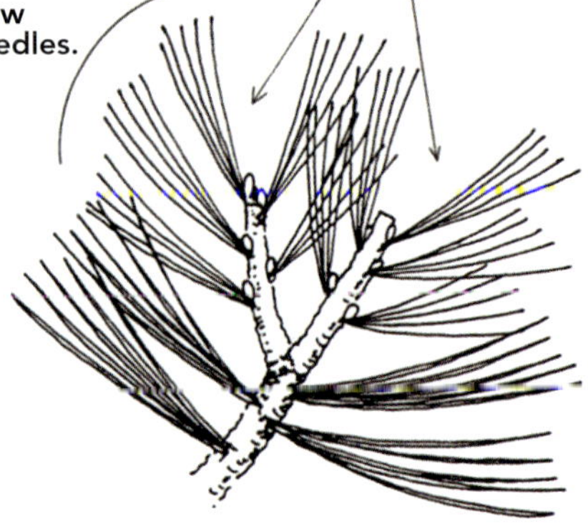

If you want to develop a well-ramified Japanese White Pine, it's crucial to understand pinching and pruning. In this chapter, Master Yosiaki simply and clearly demonstrates these techniques.

Though balancing and ramifying techniques are covered elsewhere in this book, we decided to include this chapter because of the importance of the subjects and because each artist's approach is unique.

ENCOURAGING BRANCHING

Many enthusiasts don't know how to properly pinch and prune Japanese white pines (*Pinus parviflora,* sometimes known as Japanese five-needle pine). As a result, even with the best of intentions, beautiful specimens are often ruined.

In this chapter we'll use a bonsai whose primary branches have already been defined, and explain how to pinch and prune to create a well-ramified tree. *Ramification means branching. Well-ramified branches have good secondary and tertiary branching (all the way out to fine twigs). Ramification is also sometimes used when discussing roots.*

BALANCING ENERGY

To cultivate bonsai properly, it's necessary to know how to direct energy. If a bonsai is allowed to grow freely, strong areas will become stronger and weak areas will become weaker.

The top of a tree, the section that receives the most sun and air, is usually strongest, while the tree's interior and lower branches will often be weak. *Most trees are apically dominant, which is a genetically determined tendency for a tree to put most of its energy into its apex. This has to do with the competitive race for open space and light.*

It's imperative to know how to redistribute energy from stronger to weaker areas. Two techniques involved are candle pinching and shoot pruning. If candles and shoots are allowed to grow without pinching and pruning, they unbalance the energy and compromise the design.

Once you decide where growth is needed, allow those parts of the tree to grow unchecked for one to three years. Where excessive foliage interferes with your design, begin the process of either pushing back growth (*through the techniques discussed in this chapter*) or reducing foliage.

A shoot ready for pruning.

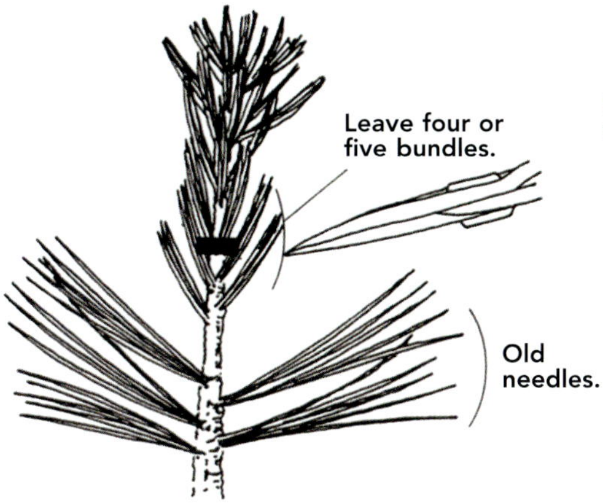

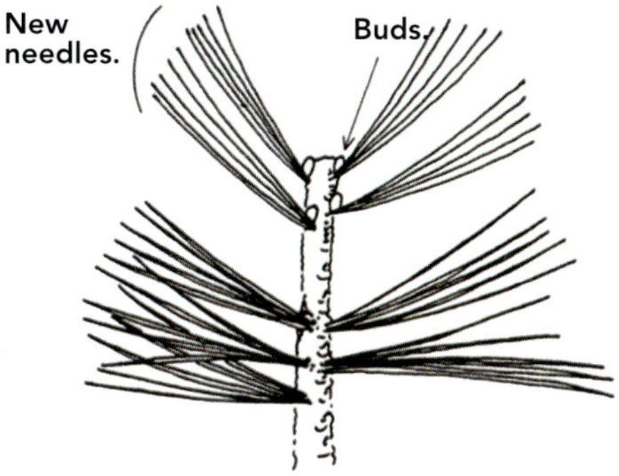

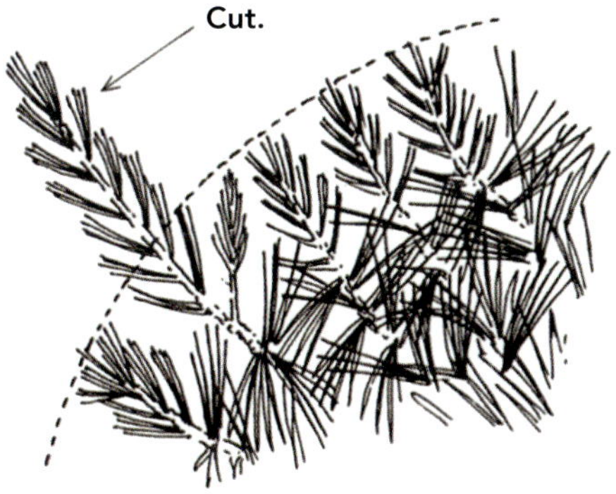

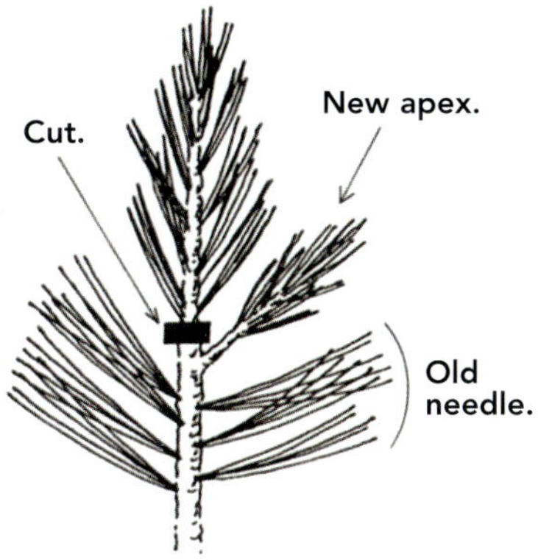

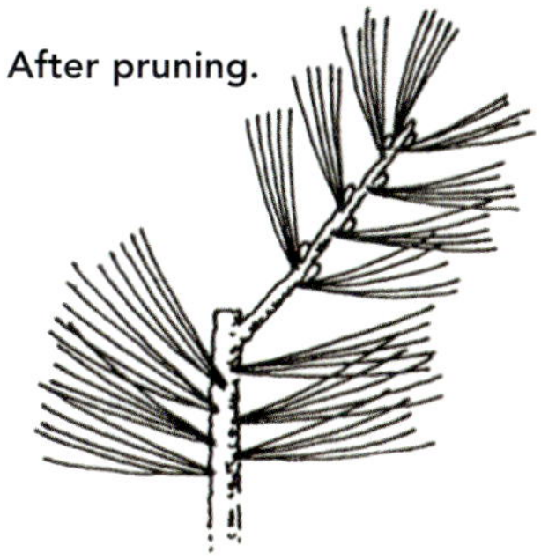

PINCHING CANDLES

The best time to pinch candles is when they are almost ready to open. Using your fingers, pinch away part of the candle. First pinch back the longest candles, then a week later pinch back the rest. The longest candles will be in the strongest part of the tree. On an established tree, pinch off about three quarters of each candle. On an immature tree, only pinch back a little. If you want a branch to lengthen, don't pinch back at all. The point where you pinch is where new buds will appear the following year.

These instructions may vary from others in this book, as techniques will vary from artist to artist. If you would like to read a another approach to candle pinching, see pages 16 & 17.

PRUNING SHOOTS

Shoot pruning is done only on the stronger sections of the tree. Prune the new shoots after the candles have opened (*candles become the new shoots*). Use sharp shears and leave four or five groups of new needles on each shoot. If a shoot is cut back to its base, it's very possible the branch will not bud again and will wither and die. Pruning shoots is not an essential operation. It is usually done when candles escape being pinched or have been left too long after pinching.

Letting a candle grow freely is an effective way to thicken a branch. With young trees, letting the candles grow into shoots and then pruning the shoots is often preferable to pinching back the candles.

BRANCH PRUNING

Trim these small branches and allow new shoots to replace them. This will help keep the tree in balance and maintain the silhouette.

FALL NEEDLE PRUNING

Before needle pruning.

After needle pruning.

PRUNING BRANCHES

In the photos above, the hardened shoots, though still quite small, are referred to as branches. Pruning branches is a task that complements shoot pruning. It is important to understand that although they are based on the same principle, they are separate jobs. Shortening outer branches causes more strength to flow to the tree's interior, refines the tree's general outline, and establishes the direction of growth of the branches. *Determining direction of growth can be summed up as cutting just above a bud or shoot that is growing in the direction you want the branch to grow.*

The best time to prune for shape, especially with strong branches, is late spring or early summer. If you have a small branch near a branch that has grown too strong for your design, cut off the strong one completely. If a branch is too long for your design, this is the best time to shorten it. *Again, be aware of the new direction of growth.*

Although most pruning is done in the spring, balancing strong and weak zones continues through the summer. In the fall energy must be realigned again, to prepare the tree for budding the following spring. While your efforts in the spring are directed at strong branches, when you prune in the fall, you should consider all the branches.

FALL NEEDLE PRUNING

The fascicles (*bundles of needles*) of the five-needle pine are delicate; if the old needles are simply pulled out, the tree might bleed excessively. Use scissors to cut off last year's needles, leaving a tiny stub above the sheath that envelopes the needles. The best time for needle pruning is early fall when the needles have matured.

Don't prune needles on weak branches; wait for them to fall off by themselves. Prune only old needles on medium strength branches. On strong branches, prune all the old needles and about half the new ones.

BUD REMOVAL

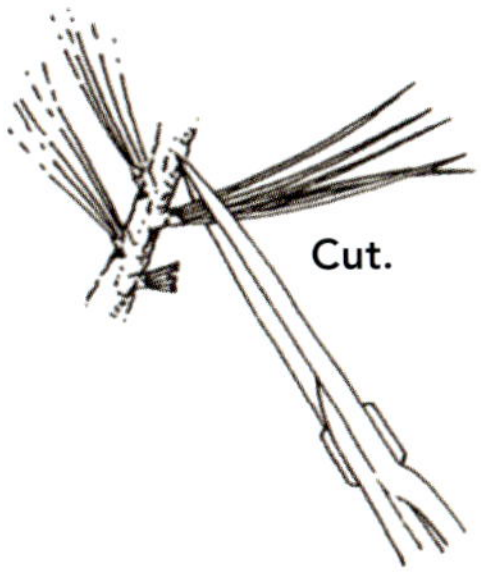

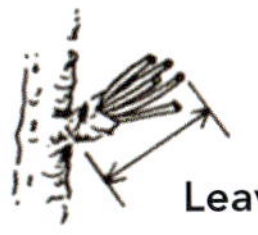

Before bud removal.

After bud removal.

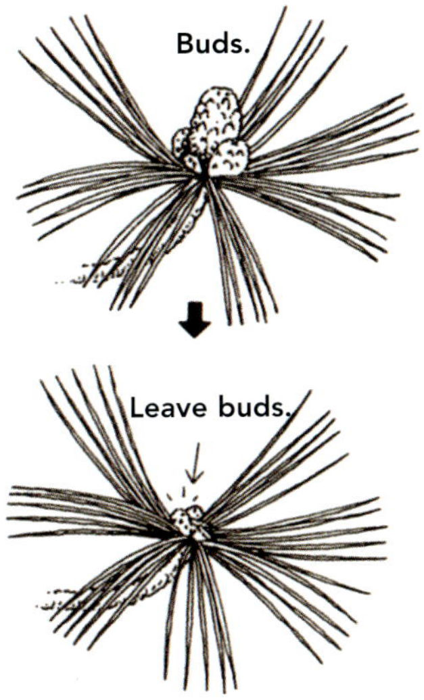

BUD REMOVAL

The best time to remove buds is mid-fall. If you leave all the buds intact, the tree will be unmanageable in the spring. Leave two buds on each shoot. On strong branches, remove the strong buds; on weak branches remove the weak buds. If you want a branch to grow, don't remove any buds. *Most people use their fingers or tweezers for bud removal.* *For more on the subject, see pages 17 and 23.*

CONCLUSION

These are the essential techniques for care of the Japanese white pine from spring to autumn. In winter, you can wire and shape. If you apply all the methods we have introduced, you will achieve the all important balancing of energy that is so essential in the development of Japanese white pines.

SUMMARY

Energy balancing is essential with pines and must be undertaken annually. If you neglect your pine, soon you will have a tree that is overgrown and unattractive.

Pinching and pruning are used to balance energy and to develop ramification.

On young trees, you can skip candle pinching and simply prune the shoots. All the other techniques offered are essential for proper energy balancing.

There are many techniques for energy balancing and needle reduction. Mr. Yosiaki's methods are quite simple and straightforward and are a good place to start.

Goyomatsu

BALANCING & REDESIGNING AN IMPORTED WHITE PINE

Michael Persiano

REDESIGNING AND DEVELOPING AN IMPORTED PINE

Despite the popularity of working with trees and shrubs native to our own area, most of us also explore working with material imported from Japan, Korea, and China. Most of these imported trees share several characteristics; they are expensive, they have significant potential and they are unrefined. One way you can accelerate development of a tree is to combine an intensive feeding program with a well-thought-out design strategy.

Japanese terms in this section include: *goyomatsu,* Japanese white pine; *shakan,* slant style tree; *ichi-no-eda,* first (lowest) branch*; ni-no-eda,* second branch; *yaku-eda,* essential or desirable branch*; tachiagari;* lower trunk from the soil line to the first branch.

In this section, we revitalize and restyle a promising 40-year-old *shakan* (slant style) Japanese white pine that was imported from Japan approximately 12 years ago.

HISTORY AND PROFILE

Goyomatsu, Japanese white pine (*Pinus parviflora)*, is a native of Japan and is characterized by smooth grayish bark on young trees, and scaly, dark gray to blackish bark on older trees. Its green to blue-green needles are curved and grow in brush-like little bundles of five (*white pines are often called five-needle pines*). In nature, or in your garden, the needles typically range from 1-1/4" to 2" (3-5 cm) in length. When grown as bonsai, the needles are usually reduced to about seventy five percent of their natural length. Japanese white pines are often grafted onto Japanese black pine trunks.

WEAKNESSES

This particular white pine was left to grow on its own for almost a decade. In order to regain its classical form, we need to reduce and restyle the crown. Some branches need to be shortened, while others need to be removed.

Before (well, almost...)
The tree as offered, with one exception. Unfortunately, I forgot to photograph before starting, so this shows the first branch after it was shortened. This tree is a fine example of imported stock with excellent potential. Though it is essentially healthy, it will require plenty of attention to strengthen the interior branches on its left side. Feeding and positioning will be critical for the next two years.

Because of poor placement, the right side of the tree has grown strong at the expense of the left side. Energy balancing measures are needed to revitalize the weak buds and to redevelop branch density. The number one branch (*ichi-no-eda*), is extremely long and in need of drastic reduction. The soil is compacted and we will need to undertake a major soil removal and replacement next year.

STRENGTHS

This white pine was masterfully grafted to a Japanese black pine trunk. The resulting *tachiagari* (lower trunk) is quite powerful. Because there are several desirable branches (*yaku-eda*), we shouldn't have too much trouble developing a strong, classical branching pattern. There are some weak inner branches that will need careful development, but this shouldn't be too much trouble. Despite a clear imbalance in energy flow, the tree is essentially healthy and capable of withstanding drastic pruning to stimulate back-budding. Finally, because of the tree's age, the bark on the scion (white pine top) is well enough developed to transition nicely with the old bark on the stock (black pine lower trunk), giving the whole tree a uniform and appealing look of age.

FROM DREAM TO REALITY

Many years ago, when I first took up the all-consuming art of bonsai, I came upon a group of interesting but pricey imported Japanese white pines. As I studied each tree, I considered how much work would be required for such an expensive tree and I resisted the urge to buy one. Instincts are often providential. Several of the trees did not acclimate and died. Others survived but lost critical limbs, leaving their once noble designs only in the minds of their distant designers. The idea that one of these survivors would find its way into my bonsai collection never crossed my mind.

Years later I revisited the same nursery and found one of the original pines. It had been allowed to grow unchecked for six years. The left side had only a few remaining branches and the apex was badly overgrown. After an hour of serious negotiation, I took possession of the tree for a fraction of the asking price.

NEW CLOTHES FOR THE EMPRESS

In the spring after acquiring the tree, its buds are thoroughly examined. The disproportionate strength of the right side signals the need to begin transferring energy to the left side. Our first step is to start pruning back the dominant growth.

The *ichi-no-eda* (first branch) is too long and needs to be reduced by approximately ten inches (*this has already occurred in the photo*). Although this is a significant reduction, the branch is still quite strong, even dominant. This is good — we want a dramatic effect.

STIMULATING BACK BUDDING

The first task is to thin out the right side. We start by combing the needles with our fingers. This gets rid of some dead and weak needles and provides an opportunity to get to know the tree. We begin to see which branches need to be eliminated and what the remaining branches might look like after they are wired and positioned. Once we become familiar with the tree and have a good idea where we're headed, we'll begin to pull needles, shorten lengthy shoots, and cut away some unnecessary shoots on the right to stimulate the tree's weakened left side.

PRUNING BACK SHOOTS

It is essential to cut back lengthy shoots to stimulate back budding. However, you must be careful not to prune too far back. Japanese white pines are less forgiving than black and red pines. If you remove all of the current season's needles, you could lose the whole branch. Be sure to leave at least four or five bundles of new needles on each shoot.

REMOVING SHOOTS

Before removing any shoots, try to picture what the branch will look like after it has been wired and shaped. If you do this, it will be easier to decide which shoots to remove. In this instance, we thin the dense three-pronged shoots by cutting away the shoot in the center.

Candle pinching.

NEEDLE PLUCKING

Needle plucking is usually done in the fall. In this case, because the needles have been neglected for years, we tackle the task immediately.

The old needles must be carefully pulled off bundle by bundle. Old needles are found closest to the trunk and tend be faded or yellowish as opposed to bright-green new needles. Take your time. If you are not careful, you run the risk of tearing the bark.

If the foliage is still dense after you pluck the old needles in the strongest zones, remove some of the new needles. Be sure not to remove too many. Again, leave at least four to five bundles on each shoot. If too many needles are removed before the new buds are formed, the branch could easily die.

You might want to experiment to see if your pine is capable of withstanding needle pulling. Use a shoot that is expendable and pull some needles. If you notice excessive sapflow (*bleeding*), consider trimming off the needles with sharp shears, leaving stubs that are approximately 1/16" long. These stubs will fall off later.

SUPERFEEDING

The author originally used the term Superfeeding 2 to distinguish this Superfeeding program from an earlier program he devised. To simplify, we decided to use the term Superfeeding instead of Superfeeding 2.

Superfeeding requires soil with excellent drainage. If you are not using fast-draining soil, **do not** Superfeed (*too much fertilizer may build up in the soil and burn the roots*). In addition, be aware that you will be promoting phenomenal root growth and will need to repot your trees at least every two years while you Superfeed.

A note on fast-draining soil. The best soils drain excess water rapidly and maintain optimal levels of water for as long as possible. This is what the author means by fast-draining soil. Optimal water retention is about 10 - 20% of capacity —air occupies the remaining 80 - 90%, which is why drainage is sometimes called aeration. Optimal water retention refers to the water-to-air ratio in which roots are able to absorb water, gasses and nutrients. This also sheds light on overwatering, which occurs when soil is seldom (or never) allowed to dry down to the optimal water-to-air ratio.

Superfeeding, phase I. Feeding immature and developing bonsai

1. Apply fertilizer cakes (*Biogold or organic pellets can be substituted*) from mid-April through August. Apply one cake for every 4 square inches of soil surface (*for more on fertilizer cakes, see page 18*).

2. Apply half-strength liquid 20-30-20 weekly from mid-April through August.

3. Apply full-strength foliage and root-drench feedings of fish emulsion every 4 weeks from April through August. Be warned that fish emulsion attracts yellow jackets!

4. Apply full-strength feedings of Roots 2 liquid with iron formula once a week on weeks 1, 3, 5, and 7 throughout May and June.

5. Apply plain Roots 2 liquid formula (without iron) once a week on weeks 2, 4, 6, and 8.

6 To prepare for winter, apply mid-month feedings of 10-60-10 in September, October and November. This provides low levels of nitrogen and potassium and high levels of phosphoric acid.

Superfeeding, phase II. Feeding mature or refined bonsai

Most trees will respond positively to phase I in one to two years. When your tree has developed enough growth to support your design goals, switch to phase II. This phase, while still aggressive, provides a maintenance level.

1. Apply full-strength foliar and root-drench feedings of fish emulsion every 4 weeks in April, May, June, July, and August.

2. Apply half strength feedings of 20-30-20 every 2 weeks during April, May, June, July, and August.

3. During May and June of year two, apply full-strength Roots 2 liquid with iron on weeks 1, 3, 5, and 7.

4. Apply fall feedings of 10-60-10 in mid-September, October, and November.

If you can't find fertilizers with the exact NPK formulas (e.g. 10-60-10) that are suggested, you can use formulas with similar ratios.

CREATING LAYERS

To create a classically styled white pine, we need to reduce and reposition the canopy. The top left branch sticks out too far and will probably need to be removed. It is never easy to cut away branches that represent decades of growth. When considering such a removal, cover the growth with a white cloth to see the impact on your design. *In the photo, hands are used instead of a cloth.* Ten years of growth are at stake, so the removal must be essential to our objective. *Many people have trouble cutting off old growth, and for good reason; you can always take it off later, but you can't put it back on. Carefully consider before you take any drastic steps. Then, when you've finally decided an old branch must go, the time for second guessing is gone. Just make your cut and move on.*

Here hands are used instead of a cloth to cover a branch the author is considering removing.

Use a concave cutter to remove the branch. After cutting, seal the wound with cutpaste and reposition branches to hide the scar. Then, like building a pagoda's tiered roof, begin to form five distinctive layers of foliage on the top third of the tree. This pagoda style works well with pines — it enhances their natural shapes and shows off the beauty of the needles.

The crown after the branch has been removed.

WIRING THE CANOPY

The lower two thirds of the tree contains several tough old branches that will only grudgingly give up their positions. To help ensure their survival after drastic repositioning, we apply raffia. The procedure is simple. The following photographs show some raffia-wrapped branches.

PROCEDURE FOR APPLYING RAFFIA

Soak the raffia in cold water for 15 minutes. Select three strands of equal length. Tie the grouping to the base of the branch, then tightly wind the raffia around the branch. If additional raffia is needed as you work your way up the branch, simply tie off the first grouping and start another three strands. Apply annealed copper wire, and then carefully bend the branch into the desired location. *If you can't use copper wire, use double, or even triple strands of heavy aluminum wire. Though aluminum is not as strong as copper, many enthusiasts use it with good results on white pines.*

Branches wrapped with raffia.

ADDITIONAL STEPS FOR DIFFICULT BENDS

If coiled wire isn't strong enough to bend a stubborn branch, lay a heavy wire spine along the length of the branch, on the outside of the proposed bend. *If this isn't enough, you can place two spines, one on the inside and one on the outside.* Then wrap the branch and the spine (or spines) together with raffia, coil your wire over the raffia and carefully bend the branch, wire spine and all.

If you think the branch needs more protection than the raffia provides, use black plastic electrical tape to provide an additional layer. The tape is quite strong and flexible and will help protect larger branches from breaking under the stress of bending. Always apply raffia first. Never apply the tape directly to the tree's bark.

PAGODA TECHNIQUE

When all the branches are wired and prepared for repositioning, you can begin to create layers of foliage using the pagoda technique. This technique can be learned through patient observation and practice. Pay careful attention to wiring and placing primary, secondary, and tertiary branches, so they all work together in a way that appears natural and harmonious. *This is especially important with pagoda style, as it's easy to end up with a stepladder effect.*

Attention to detail is important. Branches are meticulously formed into sublayers that contribute to the building of each shelf. The cumulative effect then contributes to the bonsai illusion. *This illusion is the sense of expanded space that occurs when a bonsai has the look and feel of a large tree in nature.*

Wired layers.

Removing the second branch.

A happy root system. The white is mychorrizal fungi.

Notice how the the pagoda style's distinct layers are formed.

REMOVING THE SECOND BRANCH

There is so much to appreciate with this tree, that we don't want to remove anything until we are certain that it actually detracts from the tree's potential.

The number one and number two branches are too static. To create a visual triangle between the key elements (*trunk and first and second branches*), the lower right branch needs to be removed. You can see from the photographs that the removal of this branch significantly enhances the tree's design. *Opposing branches (branches that occur at the same height on either side of the trunk) can confuse the eye as it moves up the trunk, causing it to get stuck going back and forth between the two branches. When branches move up the trunk alternately, your eye can move freely up the trunk out the first branch and back, then continue up the trunk, out the second branch, and so on.*

A GLIMPSE INTO THE FUTURE

Our six-month transformation is but a small beginning. Bonsai demands that we evolve with our trees. Things change. This evolution occurs both naturally and by a host of things we do. Ultimately, our view of bonsai and the effort we put into learning technique will determine how the evolution occurs.

Throughout the transformation, the tree is nourished by Superfeeding. You can see from the photographs that the increase in foliage density is striking for only one season's growth. While pruning, candle pinching and needle plucking are responsible for much of the progress in balancing the tree, feeding also plays an essential role.

From the front looking down — a good view of the nebari.

After the transformation.
Height 29″ (74 cm).
Trunk diameter 6″.

Plant Positioning

NINE POSSIBILITIES, AN IN-DEPTH STUDY *Artist, Masahiko Kimura*

Masahiko Kimura is considered by many to be the foremost living bonsai master. He is certainly the most famous, and is often called "The Magician." He is primarily known for his astoundingly radical transformations of difficult (if not impossible) stock into dramatic masterpieces. Kimura is also a master in the old and best sense – he consistently exhibits a deep understanding of the subtleties of classical bonsai.

This chapter presents an in-depth study of plant positioning on a collected tree. Kimura's objective is to optimize the tree's potential while preserving its wild naturalness. Seven views of the tree are explored, with discussions of the strengths and weaknesses of each. Two of the views are then chosen and the plane of each is altered, with further in-depth discussion ensuing. Finally, one view is settled upon and refined.

A bonsai's physical features present a powerful image when properly combined. A tree's roots, trunk, and branches are the raw materials, but final positioning plays a major role in how the combined elements are perceived.

Option A, the original front. Height 27" (69 cm).

The second and third branches are opposite each other and grow at the same angle.

Mr. Kimura's sketch of the trunk in option A.

A watercolor by Mr. Kimura that shows a possible future using the original front (option A).

A major transformation like this is quite risky — only a very determined person would attempt such a daring change on a mature tree. Masahiko Kimura is such a person. The bonsai in question was collected from nature over fifty years ago, thus its inherent wild character. You would never find such ruggedness in a cultivated tree.

The tree's previous owner worked on it extensively, producing thick branches and dense needles. Unfortunately, it was never exhibited or photographed, so we have no visual record of its history.

Let's look at the tree from all sides and see what it has to offer.

Option A shows the original position and front chosen by the previous owner. Although the foliage is quite attractive, this tree has a lot of unrealized potential. Our first task is to address its many defects. Viewed from the front, the apex comes forward too aggressively. The foliage is so dense that it completely hides the upper trunk and branching. The first major curve that we see (just a few inches up the trunk) is too radical at the angle shown, and the jin on the lower left is obscured by the first branch.

The first branch on the left must go. When we eliminate this branch, the tree's composition changes completely. To make sure the trunk is visible, we will also remove several other branches. If you follow the trunk up from the base, you'll see that the second and third branches grow opposite each other and come off the trunk at the same angle. This creates a visual conflict and needs to be remedied.

Since our goal is to expose more of the trunk and eliminate the conflict created by opposing branches, the second branch must go. Now the third branch becomes the new first branch (primary branch). It is too small now and needs to grow some. When we remove the first two branches, everything changes and a new pattern is established for the remaining branches.

Because we have left a void on the right of the tree, we'll bring down a back branch to fill in a bit. This will also help soften the trunk's overly dramatic curve. As we go up the the trunk, the remaining branches will follow the same rhythm of separation and inclination.

As Kimura's watercolor reflects, we have coaxed a new shape out of the old tree, while keeping in mind the vision of its previous owner and our own intuition about the tree's hidden potential. This more open look accentuates the tree's maturity, which is its greatest asset.

Now let's see what happens if we look at the tree from a number of perspectives:

Option B.

Now you can see the taper at the base of the trunk more clearly. However, the nebari is no good from this angle and the first curve of the trunk doesn't show because it moves towards the front and is almost parallel to the ground. Also, the section of trunk after the second curve is not shown to its best advantage — it is almost parallel to the ground and is somewhat straight and monotonous.

Option C.

From this angle the taper on the lower trunk is good and you can now see the first curve. However, the rest of the trunk is a mess. A very long monotonous stretch parallels the ground and also hides some curves that are among the tree's most outstanding features. Furthermore, the nebari is no good at all from this angle.

Option D.

From this view the trunk appears thin at the base and thicker higher up. This reverse taper is completely unacceptable. Also, the apex leans towards the back (a slight lean to the front is best) and the jin at the base of the trunk is hidden. The only advantage this front presents is a much improved view of the nebari.

Option E.

Here the view of the base of the trunk and the jin is excellent, much better than with the previous fronts. There are still two major defects: the lower section of trunk comes forward and the apex slants back rather than slightly forward.

Option F.

As in option E, this view of the base of the trunk emphasizes the tree's naturalness and wild beauty. However, the jin is too long and is visually dominant, and the trunk slants almost straight back, away from the viewer.

Option G.

This view presents a wild, rugged image, but, as in B and C, the trunk has a long monotonous stretch that runs parallel to the ground. Because the base of the trunk is so strong, this fault becomes even more apparent.

Option H.

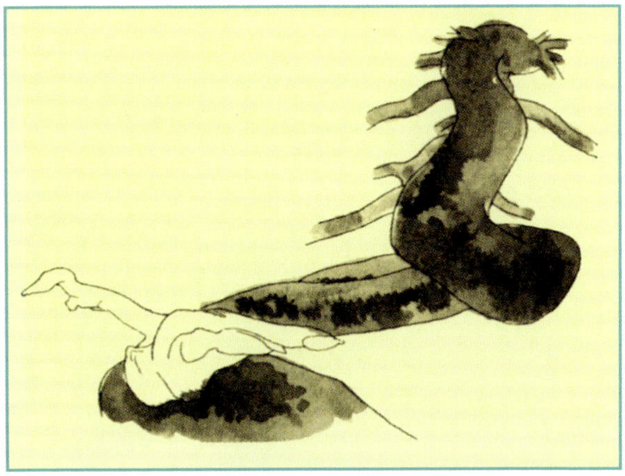

In this case, the jin points aggressively towards your eye. If corrected, this view would feel natural, except for one unredeemable defect — the top of the trunk grows straight and upright, in conflict with the flowing curves along the rest of the trunk.

B-1. The same as B, but with a different planting angle. The trunk is no longer horizontal.

If we take into consideration the tree's original design, it is clear that the front should be option A. It presents the best *nebari* (exposed surface roots), *tachiagari* (lower trunk), *yaku-eda* (essential branches) and overall trunk shape and movement (the overall style is *moyogi*, or informal upright). But this is also the easiest path to take. It might be more interesting to take another look, as this tree has many possibilities that have been obscured by its original planting position.

If you step back and consider other possibilities, many faults can be corrected, and characteristics that enhance the tree's natural ruggedness can be emphasized in ways we have yet to consider. However, if we end up with a tree that looks younger or tamer, our work will be a failure. *This is a common beginner's mistake. In attempting to conform to basic rules and conventional styles, we may inadvertently remove or hide the very features that make a tree powerful and unique.*

Let's see what happens if we change the planting angle with the help of wooden wedges. We'll start with option B from our previous analysis (see B-1).

Suddenly you have the impression of a much taller tree. The trunk's variations in thickness go almost unnoticed, and the lower trunk is no longer parallel to the ground and seems much more harmonious and dynamic.

Another advantage to B-1 over the original B is, with B the branches were lower and visually interfered with the motion of the trunk's first wide sweeping curve. Now simply by changing the planting angle, the sweeping curve is not slowed down by distracting branches.

One problem with the solution shown in B-1 is the first branch (*on the left*) now comes straight out toward the front. It also partially hides the jin. If we choose this solution, we need to remove this branch or convert it into a short jin. (*see Kimura's B-1 sketch*).

Now take a look at F-1. In F, the main defect was that the line of the trunk grew sharply toward the back and then came forward. By changing the planting position, this defect almost disappears. Now the hump of the curve is not so distracting.

With this solution, the trunk seems taller and the curves considerably more harmonious. Best of all, the tree's original ruggedness has been preserved (*see Kimura's F-1 sketch*).

B-1 sketch. The future of the tree.

WHICH FRONT IS BEST?

We still haven't decided. Two possibilities (*B-1 and F-1*) have positive features with only one real negative. In both, the apex tilts away from us towards the back. However, this problem can be solved in both cases by further adjustments of the planting angles. *Followed by some pruning and the application of a little wire.* Because Mr. Kimura can visualize what the apex will look like after correction, he now knows that F-1 is the most appropriate front. The tree's wild character is more obvious than with B-1, and the lower trunk and jin show to the best possible advantage.

With this latest correction, the trunk has a very pleasing soft and graceful movement. At the same time, the ruggedness of the trunk's base, bark, jin and other natural features haven't been lost.

The original B sketch, before the planting angle was changed.

However, one job remains. The tree still has so many branches that you can't clearly see the graceful shape of the trunk. Some will have to be removed. Start with the first branch that grows toward the front. To avoid creating visible scars, jin every branch you remove. Later you can remove any jin you don't want.

F-1. As soon as the planting position is changed, the trunk's curves become much more evident.

CREATING A JIN

It's important when making a jin to leave some fine branches coming off the jin. This makes for a more natural look.

When creating jin from non-essential branches (*imi-eda),* use the following six-part technique:

1. Place your concave cutter at the point where the branch connects to the trunk and carefully twist the cutter back and forth to cut into the bark, without cutting through the branch.

2. To make it easy to peel, lightly crush the bark along the length of the jin with your pliers.

3. Carefully peel away the bark using pliers. On fine twigs you can use your fingernails to gently scrape away the bark.

4. To create a natural look, use pliers to splinter the ends of the jin.

5. Apply cut paste where the jin connects to the trunk to minimize bleeding.

6. After allowing the branches to dry for several days, apply a coat of lime-sulfur solution. If you want more contrast between the jin and bark, you can mix white watercolor paint into the lime-sulfur. *The primary purpose of lime-sulfur is to protect the dead wood from fungus that causes rot. Without lime-sulfur, most jin and shari would simply rot away.*

CONTINUING UP THE TRUNK

Now look at the new first branch on the left. It is too long and has too much visual weight. While it is okay for this branch to hide a portion of the trunk, since it needs to have some strength and distinctive character, some of it still needs to be removed. Start with the secondary branch that grows toward the trunk. When this is gone, further lighten the branch by thinning some of the excess tertiary branching. Leave most of the part that grows toward the back to help fill an open space and give the tree more depth.

The remaining branches are well placed, but the crown feels too dense and compact. You can create a sense of movement and rhythm by adding space to the composition. To accomplish this, jin a branch on the upper left part of the trunk.

A scar on the second branch (the first branch on the right) shows there was a previous attempt to force it into a lower position. This is precisely what you want to do — it needs to come down so that its foliage is located about one-third of the way up the trunk. This prevents the trunk from seeming excessively bare and creates an overall sense of balance. *Triangulation and dividing space into*

F-1 sketch. The future of the tree.

The original F sketch, before the planting angle was changed.

thirds are often used in bonsai and other arts to create a natural and pleasing sense of balance.

To avoid breaking the branch when you bring it down, protect the old wound with raffia.

When Mr. Kimura finishes moving this branch down, its lower pad is below the first branch on the left. Even though it originates above the first branch on the left, visually it is now the tree's primary branch.

The shape of the branches should complement the shape of the trunk. Since the trunk is not ordinary, the branches should not be ordinary either.

Since the trunk slants to the right, the first branch on the left adds visual stability. You need to prune it some more to add more movement. Leave a little bit toward the back that will peek out on the right. This helps bring the visual weight of the tree towards the center.

Throughout this exercise we've changed the tree's position many times. The same goes for our choice of the first branch. Being able to adapt as you go along demands flexibility. You must let yourself be guided by intuition as much as technique, as each change creates a new situation that challenges your imagination.

Now let's return to technique. With all the new wounds you've created, you must apply cutpaste on every cut and at the base of each jin. This protects against disease and dehydration.

The work is almost finished. Repositioning the branches of the crown to reconcile them with the shape and inclination of the trunk and the branches, particularly the first branch, is the final task. The most important branches are the first three, and success depends on how well they work together and how well they work with the trunk. The first and back branches have been worked already, leaving just the second right branch to reposition.

You need to reduce this branch so it doesn't cover the first branch. Adequate spacing is necessary to clearly define the three main branches. The space between the branches must harmonize with the movement of the trunk. Without some open space, you won't be able to see the lines of the trunk or the branches. Where there is adequate space, pleasing curves and other important features are more evident. Where there is not enough space, trees tend to look immature and uninteresting.

PROTECT WOUNDS BEFORE BENDING

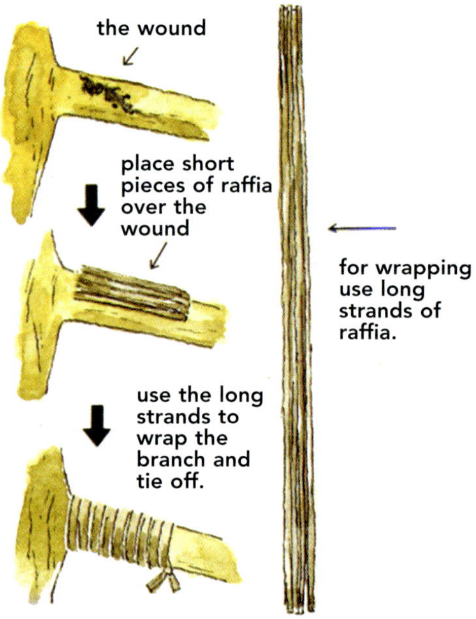

CHANGING A BRANCH'S POSITION

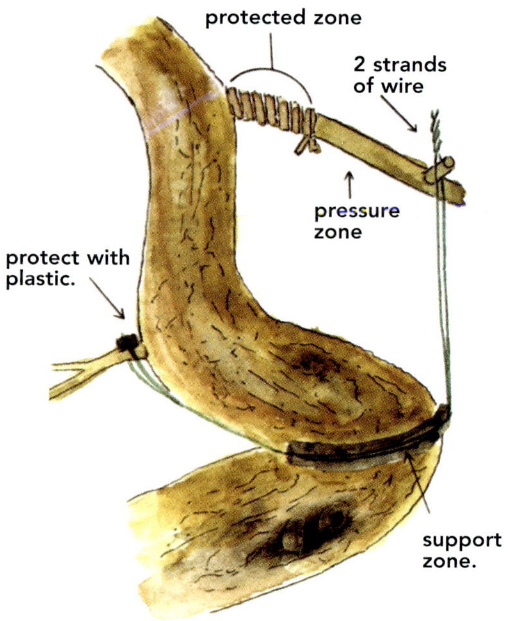

To move the branch down, insert a short heavy piece of wire (a nail or short dowel will work) between the two strands of wire and twist. Go slowly and in stages. This gives the branch a chance to adjust as you go.

CREATING JIN

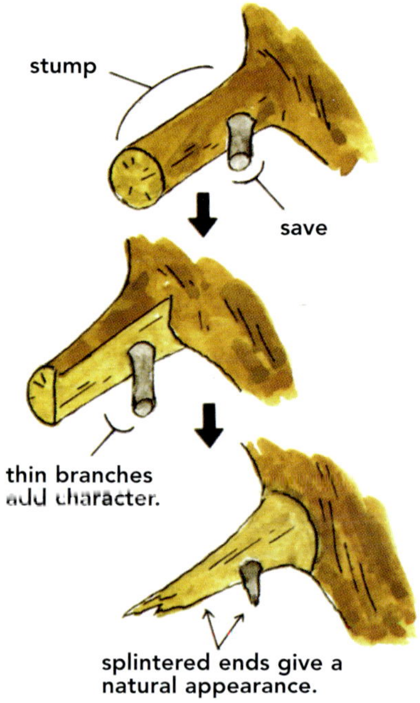

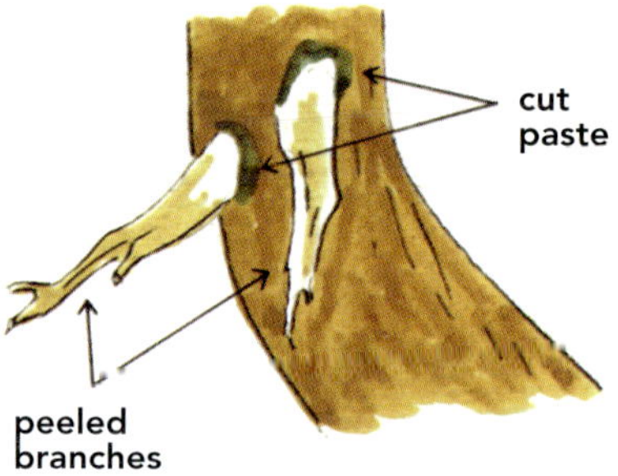

The apex and branches are starting to shape up, but there is still some refining to do.

Now the lower trunk (*tachiagari*) looks much better.

A secondary branch that comes off the first branch still partially hides the trunk.

The secondary branch is cut back part way, leaving a long stub (in this photo it looks as though Kimura is going to cut off the whole branch).

The stub will be used as a jin.

Now, with just the stub, you have a better view of the trunk.

Stripping the bark off the stub.

A close-up of the jinned area. Note the natural appearance of the trunk and bark.

Below. After the cutpaste and lime-sulphur has been applied..

When all the main branches are wired, we begin to change their position.

Front.

Take care to allow some space between the main branches.

Right.

Back.

Left.

THE ROOTS

The last phase is adapting the rootball to the new planting position. This should be simple, unless there are too many thick horizontal roots. Since the branches and foliage were very dense, the roots should be abundant and fine. On the side you are going to raise, you'll have to remove some surface soil and roots. On the side you're going to lower, only the bottom roots need to be removed. Once you've evaluated the condition of the roots, you can carry out the last positioning adjustments.

Notice how the jin flows into a small shari on the trunk and how its tip almost reaches the first branch. These small features create delightful effects that give the tree that little extra something.

The total height of the tree is still 27", the same as it was when we started. The transformation is a success and Mr. Kimura is quite pleased.

When you've finished with the top, begin to reshape the rootball to fit with the new planting position.

You need to eliminate the upper part of the rootball on the side that is elevated, while removing the lower part of the rootball on the other side.

Before.

The round drum pot suits the flowing lines of the tree perfectly. An ordinary bonsai has become a masterpiece.

Primary Branch

SELECTING THE BEST ONE

Susumo Sudo and Masahiko Kimura

A

B

Selecting the right primary branch can mean the difference between a powerful or mediocre design. While there is usually one superior option, other viable options almost always exist.

Many important elements of a bonsai might go unnoticed with a casual viewing. Without a doubt, the most important element is the trunk, which shapes the character of the whole tree. Obviously, branches are important too, as they emphasize the trunk and strongly influence the overall feel of the tree.

Because bonsai generally have fewer branches than trees growing in the wild, each branch is very important. The primary branch is crucial — not only is it the strongest and most visible branch, it powerfully effects the way the trunk is perceived and is the reference point for choosing and shaping all the other branches. Designing a bonsai without selecting the primary branch early in the process can be very difficult.

In most cases the primary branch is the lowest branch, though occasionally this is not the case. This is why the Japanese use two distinct terms: *ichi-no-eda* (lowest branch, or first branch), and *sashi-eda* (strongest branch).

In the first section of this chapter, Mr. Susumo Sudo uses digital imaging to explore several options for choosing a primary branch on a Japanese white pine.

In the second part, Mr. Masahiko Kimura affects a dramatic change by a slight angle change, some much needed thinning, and removing the original primary branch.

The two terms, ***primary branch*** *and* ***primary branches****, are easy to confuse. The primary branch is always the main, or strongest branch, and is usually the lowest branch (often called the first branch). The term* ***primary branches*** *refers to all the branches growing off the trunk. These are distinguished from secondary and tertiary branches. Secondary branches grow off primary branches and tertiary branches grow off secondary branches (and so forth).*

SUSUMO SUDO

Which bonsai is best?

Pick your favorite from photos A-J. Then look at the actual bonsai by Susumo Sudo. Try to understand the thinking behind his design.

The most powerful demonstration of the primary branch's importance is the bonsai itself. This series of photographs shows the primary branch in various places and presents an analysis of how it relates to the overall design.

What's the best position for the primary branch?

Mr. Sudo selected position E, but there are several alternatives that merit serious consideration.

When working with a bonsai, think of it as a complete entity with a single objective — communicating harmony and beauty. All of the elements of a bonsai come together to produce a single impression. In light of this, an old tree should not have young branches at the base; they undermine the expression of age and confuse the viewer.

First, let's analyze the qualities of this tree. The overall effect is an old tree in the bunjin (*literati*) style. Bunjin are tall trees that usually feature relatively thin trunks with lots of movement, and most of the branches on the upper third of the tree.

This tree has an elegant and mature beauty. The curves of the trunk are smooth; the tree is somewhat thin and tall and has very few branches. The shari (*dead wood that occurs on the trunk, sometimes called driftwood*) on the lower trunk and the various jin (*dead branches*) add character.

Because the tree is leaning to the right, you can assume that's where it receives the most sunlight. The largest jin is found on the opposite (*shaded*) side, which is where most dead branches appear on trees found in nature.

The upper branches are young, so they don't impart an impression of age — a defect only time will correct. Mr. Sudo keeps in mind a basic bunjin rule: if you want to create the feeling of age, the branches, like the trunk, should be elegant and somewhat bare. *Young trees tend to have branches with little definition and dense foliage.*

You must take a lot into account when selecting the location of the primary branch: the direction of growth, the shape and features of the trunk, the location of the other branches and the height of the tree. All these aspects influence the placement and shape of the primary branch.

Normally the first element to consider is the first branch, but in this instance, the process for designing the tree is reversed in order to emphasize the importance of the primary branch. Do you still think your selection is the best? Think about it again, while seriously considering Mr. Sudo's reasons for selecting option E.

Option A. The trunk grows to the right while the branch grows to the left. This is no good. If a trunk grows toward the right, it's because the sun shines more fully on that side. When attempting to cultivate a natural look, it's not logical that the first branch, which is the densest and the longest, should grow in a spot where the sunlight is weak. It's also growing too low on the trunk, making the tree appear unbalanced. *The notion that the primary branch should grow on the side that the trunk leans toward contradicts what you will sometimes hear and see from other teachers. Ultimately there are no fixed rules, just people's perceptions and ideas.*

Option B. This option is debatable. The tree appears unnatural without the primary branch. Perhaps if the trunk were thinner and the planting angle were modified to incline the tree a little more to the right, this version might be good. As it is, without the primary branch, it doesn't convey enough feeling of age.

Option C. The height of the primary branch is about right — it doesn't interfere with the branch immediately above, and there is enough space for the lower portion of the trunk. But, as already mentioned (*option A*), it's completely unnatural for the main branch to grow from a spot that does not receive strong sunlight. Eliminating the thickest jin from the tree also diminishes the tree's character and the appearance of age.

Option D. As with A and C, the location on the shady side is unnatural. Also, it's completely wrong for a tall thin tree to have its first branch so low on the trunk. Remember, in the bunjin style, branches are usually located on the upper third of the tree. *Actually, Mr. Sudo's choice is less than two-thirds of the way up the trunk.*

F

G

H

Option E. This is the option selected by Mr. Sudo. The others may have some merit when you consider all the points, but option E is the best.

Option F. The branch is on the correct side of the tree. Its height on the trunk is also good. However, the jin on the left has been eliminated. Without the jin, the tree appears younger, and worse still, it appears unbalanced; as though it is falling to the right.

Option G. This option might appear okay at first glance, but it's not. Not only does the primary branch cover the two attractive small jin, it's also too close to the top of the tree, creating a bunched up effect.

Option H. The branch is located on the correct side, but it's still too high. It overpowers the jin immediately above it, and diminishes the effect of the larger jin on the left side of the tree. Though this solution is better than some, if you were to use it, the foliage on the primary branch would need to be reduced to reveal the branch's structure and lighten up the top of the tree. *This is the one I (WS) chose. It seems more in keeping with bunjin principles and appears well balanced, provided the foliage is reduced as Mr. Sudo suggests.*

Option I. Such a dense branch would never grow from so much deadwood (*shari*). It's also much too low on the trunk.

Option J. Though it is a bit higher than option I, it still has the same problems.

As you can see, the location of the first branch strongly influences the impression a tree conveys and also suggests the nature of its environment. The lesson you can draw from this exercise is that bonsai is an idealized tree growing in nature. If we understand and are able to apply this notion, then our bonsai will continue to improve.

In order to really understand bonsai as an expression of a tree growing in nature, all the elements must contribute to the overall effect. You need to take everything into consideration — the trunk, the primary branch, the rest of the branches growing off the trunk, as well as secondary and tertiary branches, fine twigs and tips, foliage, jin and shari, the apex, the roots, the bark, the pot, the surface of the soil — every single feature is important.

Still, it's undeniable that some elements are more critical to the composition than others. They immediately stand out, even when you see a bonsai as a unified whole. These critical elements are: surface roots, trunk and primary branch. This exercise is an attempt to help us think logically about the primary branch.

Mr. Sudo often says "If you cannot logically explain your choice, it is possible you are mistaken."

The actual tree designed by Susumu Sudo, in a handmade bunjin pot. Height 27″ (69 cm). Notice how a guy-wire is used to pull down the first left branch.

Before restyling. Height 34" (86 cm)

MASAHIKO KIMURA

Mr. Kimura acquired this old white pine in January 1981. He was particularly taken by its rough old trunk and the fact that it is growing on its own roots, even though the design is mediocre. *In Japan, almost all white pines are grafted onto black pine root stock to utilize the black pine's vigorous roots and its beautifully fissured bark – white pine bark is also quite beautiful, it just requires much more time to develop.*

A unique quality of this tree is its quite compact growth, which is not usually characteristic of unmaintained Japanese white pines. Unattended trees normally develop unsightly leggy growth. If the problem is not caught in time, it can be extremely difficult to reclaim the tree for bonsai.

Another outstanding feature of this old bonsai is the near perfect silhouette formed by its well-arranged branches. Still, in many ways it appears to be more bush than bonsai. An excellent opportunity to show off the majestic old trunk is being wasted while a perpetual state of youth is being maintained. In nature, foliage becomes more open and trunks and branches become more exposed over time.

Since old pines don't easily generate new growth, Mr. Kimura isn't able to prune too much at first. As a result, the reshaping process takes a full two years.

Carefully compare the old tree's appearance before and after reshaping. You can see changes in the three distinct areas that are the most important elements of bonsai design: the roots, the trunk and the branches. Notice how the planting level is now lower and the roots are growing solidly into the soil without swelling above the rim of the pot. Also, notice how the planting angle is inclined a little toward the right, adding more movement to the trunk.

More work is done with the branches than any other element. In addition to changing the angles of the branches coming off the trunk by inclining the planting position, the foliage is considerably reduced, exposing more trunk and the bases of the branches. This allows you to see and appreciate the basic structure of the tree. *One of the most important things any beginner needs to learn is how to expose the structure of a tree. Until we learn to do this, our plants are simply bushes.*

Mr. Kimura decides to remove the first branch on the right because it creates an unbalanced feel. Now the new primary branch (the first left branch) works much better with the other branches, resulting in a more balanced and harmonious effect. Here's the proof: put your hand over the primary branch in the photo of the finished tree, and you'll notice that the tree still retains a natural, balanced appearance. Now cover the primary branch in the before photo. Balance is lost and the tree looks completely unnatural.

The primary branch doesn't always have to be obvious, but where it leads the rest of the branches must follow.

After restyling. Height 31″ (79 cm).

Multiple Trunk Bonsai

THREE BONSAI, THREE PERSPECTIVES

Artist: Masahiko Kimura

Masahiko Kimura styles tree multiple trunk white pines. In the first he demonstrates how a collected pine can be transformed into a work of art while violating one of bonsai's basic rules; he allows trunks to cross. All three restylings present valuable examples of how a master works with technique and vision to achieve balance, depth and perspective.

Clump style Japanese white pine just after it was collected. Height 35" (89 cm).

FIRST TREE

The principal problem with this tree, a clump style planting, is lack of direction or unity. Each trunk seems to have its own agenda, with little relationship to any overall form.

The perspective is less of a problem, with a strong primary trunk as well as several other trunks that work well with the primary trunk in scale and balance (with one exception).

If the various trunks had grown closer together, the arrangement would have fewer problems. As it is, the diverging trunk lines start at a point well below the soil level and present some difficulty. Another issue is the two trunks that are almost identical in thickness.

Mr. Kimura realizes that he has to inspect the roots to see if it is possible to expose the point at which the trunks diverge. If it's possible, then one of the most challenging problems can be solved.

Little by little the master cleans the soil from the rootball. As he works his way down, something entirely unexpected and unwanted suddenly shows up — beetle larvae. It turns out to be a stroke of luck that Kimura decided to inspect the roots. Had he waited a few more days, it might have been too late.

Mr. Kimura starts by inspecting the roots to see if he can expose the trunks beneath the soil.

An unexpected and uninvited guest shows up. Beetle larvae.

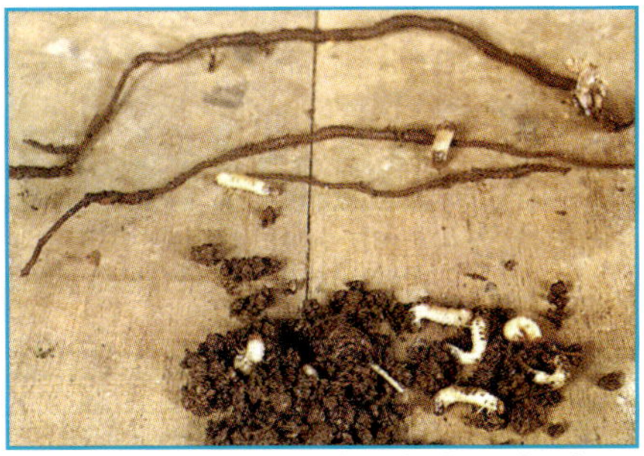

It's good Mr. Kimura decided to check the roots. Otherwise the tree was doomed.

A very heavy root is removed.

The stump from the trunk that was removed. A small bud is kept at its base for a future trunk.

A pot is chosen and tried out.

Securely in its new pot with fresh soil.

The transplanting is completed. It's time to style the top. The top is usually styled before transplanting, but in this case, Kimura needed to look at the roots before starting.

To check how active and voracious the larvae are, Kimura places some in a container with soil and a few roots. Four days later, when he checks the container, the thick roots are intact but all the small feeder roots have been devoured. Trees don't stand a chance without feeder roots. Certain death is the only possible result. It's very important to watch for beetles, particularly at the end of the summer when they lay eggs that quickly hatch into voracious larvae. *The beatles referred to are common in Japan and may not occur in your area. However, there are any number of insects that can damage roots and it always pays to be on the lookout.*

The first step is to decide which primary branches on the main trunk need to be removed.

After pruning the main trunk. Notice how most of the branches are on the outsides of the curves.

Because the roots were damaged, Mr. Kimura decides on a larger pot that will give new roots more space to grow. *A pot that is larger than an ideal show pot is sometimes called a training pot. The one danger with pots that are on the large size is overwatering, as pockets of soil may stay too soggy. You can avoid this by making sure your soil has good drainage and by using training pots that are only about half again as large (in volume) as the eventual show pot.*

In multiple trunk arrangements, the trees should be different heights and thicknesses. *Though many bonsai artists make this point, in fact, in nature, and sometimes in bonsai, there are forests that consist of trees that are fairly uniform in size. Bonsai plantings with numerous trees – 13 or more – are sometimes started with seedlings that are the same age and more or less the same size.*

In nature the oldest tree is the tallest and thickest. The younger trees are shorter and thinner and their shape is determined in part by the primary tree; shade from the primary tree influences the growth of the rest of the trees.

In this case, two of the trunks are almost the same thickness. Because group plantings need one primary tree, Mr. Kimura selects the central tree and removes the one on the left. Actually, instead of totally removing it, he leaves a bud growing on its base that will develop into another trunk. Then there will be an odd number of trunks. The remaining trunks, eight in number, plus the small bud, will make up the arrangement. *Japanese (and other) bonsai artists, prefer odd numbers.*

Wiring and separating the trunks.

After thinning the apex and secondary branches.

All the trunks are wired and ready to be positioned.

The positions are established.

The trunks are still a tangled mess.

The trunks and the branches are now in place .

The transformation to a bunjin clump style bonsai is complete. Notice the crossing trunks — a taboo is broken. Height 37" (94 cm).

SECOND TREE

This Japanese white pine was collected from nature. The tree is a *netsuranari*, or sinuous root bonsai (*a number of trunks growing from the same surface root*). Though both *kabudachi* (clump style) and *netsuranari* are common with white pines, many enthusiasts hesitate to use them, as the fixed positions of the trunks makes styling quite challenging. This is particularly true with sinuous root trees.

Because the trunks are already established, their basic shapes and directions are difficult or impossible to change *(this is especially true of the larger trunks).* As a result, the problems of perspective, depth and scale need to be solved by changing the front, changing the pot, changing the potting placement and angles, removing some trunks, minor modifications of the remaining trunks, and working with the branches.

Perspective and balance are realized in this tree by changing the front and carefully shaping the branches. The play between positive and negative space preserves a sense of depth and gradation, and the gracefully curving trunks slowly ascend from the edge of the composition to the tip of the dominant tree. The short well-spaced branches enhance the scale of the design.

Before

After.

Before.

After.

THIRD TREE

Mr. Kimura's transformation of this Kabudachi (clump style) planting consists of the following simple, basic tasks: eliminating unnecessary branches, reducing foliage, wiring and repositioning the smaller trunks and many of the branches, shaping all the trunks and branches, and repotting. No trunks are eliminated and the shape of the planting doesn't change dramatically. Still, the effect is dramatic, as the tree is transformed from an ordinary potential bonsai to an elegant work of art.

Though a number of obvious and subtle changes contribute to this masterful transformation, it is easy to miss the lines of movement along the foliage.

One line slowly descends, like a tiered waterfall, from the tip of the apex down to the foliage on the large trunk on your left. It continues down to the foliage on the smaller trunk between the two larger trunks, ultimately bringing your eye back to the main trunk. *This is a masterful stroke that enhances awareness of the foliage and its relationship with the spine of the composition (the main trunk).*

On the other side, the foliage flows down from the apex of the primary tree to the apex of the large secondary tree on the right. From there, it gently drops from tier to tier down the right edge of the planting to the empty space below. This draws our attention to the pleasing concave line that flows from the right hand edge of the pot and up the right hand trunk. Looking at the parts in this way helps us to better see the whole tree.

Like the first planting, the most distinctive feature of this one is the harmonious play of form and space. Kimura resists the all too common temptation to fill in most of the available space and conveys the impression of tall trees against the vast blue sky.

JAPANESE TERMS

Kabudachi, *(clump style), literally means 'multi-trunk,' and is a single tree with one crown and two or more trunks. What distinguishes kabudachi from forest style (yose-ue) is that all the trunks grow from the same root system and therefore are parts of the same tree.*

Netsuranari *(sinuous root style) is a variation of kabudachi style that occurs fairly commonly with Japanese white pines. This is where several trunks emanate from a single sinuous surface root. This style sometimes occurs in nature when a trunk puts out a root that grows across the top of a rock. As this root meanders along, it puts out new trunks of its own. These trunks are considered offsprings of the parent (primary) trunk.*

Netsuranari should be distinguished from ikada (raft style), another variation of kabudachi. Ikada occurs when a fallen (or placed) trunk lies along the ground (or just below the ground) and eventually becomes a root that pushes up a row of new trunks. In order for this to occur, the original trunk must retain all or part of its original root system until it can push out new roots. In other words, you can't simply cut off a trunk and lay it along (or under) the ground and expect it to develop into a ikada.

Bunjin *(literati style), also called bunjin-gi, was originally inspired by Sumi ink drawings of rugged old pines growing in the most inhospitable areas of remote Chinese mountains.*

Though it is difficult to say anything too definite about bunjin, as it often typifies a certain freedom that defies categorization, here's our attempt: Bunjin is often distinguished by relatively long, thin trunks marked by unusual and often dramatic movement. Like the trunk, the sparse branches, which tend to be on the upper third of the tree, are often dramatically and unpredictably shaped. Precisely what you would expect on trees that cling to life in rugged, inhospitable terrains. Bunjin are usually planted in low round (or nearly round) pots. Drum pots (see the tree on the previous page) are often used, as are rustic handmade pots. The overall feeling of a good bunjin is an almost contradictory sense of ruggedness and elegance.

SUMI

Mr. Kimura has never before deliberately crossed trunks. So why does he do it now? When asked, he responds that he has been profoundly influenced by the beauty of sumi paintings and that the old sumi masters weren't concerned about trunks crossing or not crossing. Just natural beauty.

Sumi has long been an inspiration for bonsai artists, with its impressionistic representations that express a profound appreciation for the natural beauty which lies at the heart of bonsai. Many classic bonsai have been directly derived from sumi paintings. This influence is particularly evident in the bunjin style, where sumi seems to be a natural medium for capturing the simplicity, grace and ruggedness of some of nature's most dramatic trees.

Rock Planting

FROM A TO ZUISHO *Artist: Mikio Oshima*

Studying the raw materials.

Five years after planting. Height: 26 inches (66cm).

Immediately after planting.

Styling begins one year later.

Mixing the soil. Use 60% humus, 40% akadama dust, mix well, add water and mix again.

Making fissures in the rock.

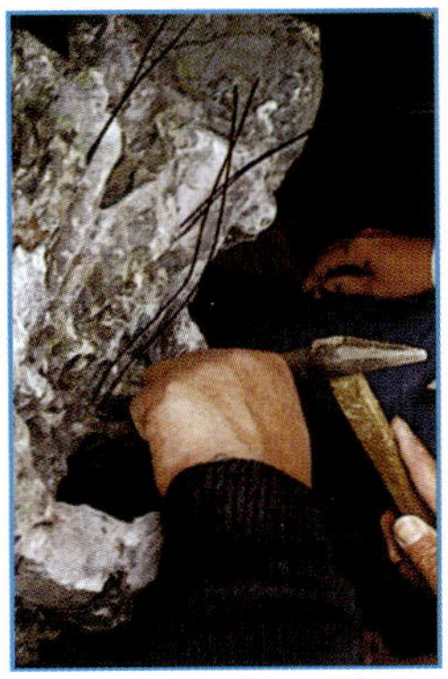

Pressing lead weights into the fissures with a chisel.

Applying epoxy.

Though rock planting is suitable to any number of plant varieties, the Zuisho Japanese white pine has long been a favorite, as it looks natural in rugged, rocky landscapes and adapts well to the demands imposed by precarious perches with limited amounts of soil. When done well, the illusion is that of a full-sized old pine growing on a high rocky cliff deep inside some remote mountain range.

In this chapter, Mikio Oshima covers what you need to be successful with rock plantings, including: choosing plants, shaping plants, making the soil, fastening the plants to the rock, selecting rocks and much more.

CHOOSING YOUR MATERIAL

The size and dimensions of the stone should determine the size of the trees. For a medium-sized stone, two-year old plants are suitable. Choose trees with dense buds. Good *nebari (surface roots)* and thick trunks aren't so important, since these will develop after the trees are established on the rock. *Zuishos are not always easy to find. If you can't find them, other varieties of Japanese white pine can also be used, though the Zuisho is particularly suitable because of its very short dense needles and short internodes.*

SOIL MIX

Since you transplant very infrequently with bonsai rooted on rocks, you must use a soil mix with abundant nutrients and enough density to stay in place during watering. *When you grow bonsai in pots, you need to repot every one to five years. With bonsai on rocks, the intervals are much greater. We've seen trees that have been on rocks for over twenty years without transplanting.*

Use a mixture of 60% humus and 40% very fine akadama (*or clay if you don't have akadama*). Mix both ingredients thoroughly while still dry, or else the mix won't be uniform. Add water and blend until the mixture has a paste-like consistency.

PREPARING THE ROCK

It's essential that you bind the trees firmly to the rock. Short lengths of aluminum wire attached to the rock are the best way to hold the trees in place.

You can use an epoxy putty to attach the wire to the rock. Many such products are readily available in most parts of the world and are easily applied to rock (*we've had good luck with Superglue and other similar cyanoacrylate glues*). Start by tearing off enough putty to secure several pieces of wire. Then knead the two-part putty in your hand until well mixed. Next press small mounds of the epoxy onto the rock, and then attach several lengths of aluminum wire. Epoxy's holding power is incredible, so it's unlikely it will ever separate from the rock.

Another option is to drill holes into the rock and insert concrete screws, leaving at least a quarter inch for attaching the wire. Wrap the base of the wire onto the screw, and you are ready to proceed with the planting. You can also epoxy lead weights with wire attached into fissures in the rocks (see photos).

Adding soil completes the preparation.

PLANNING YOUR ARRANGEMENT

Because you will be using young slender material, the shape of the trunk and branches can easily be modified later. If the trees are rooted on the rock in the fall, they can be shaped with wire the following spring.

Consider very carefully where to place each tree, as it is very difficult to make changes once the trees are wired into place.

Plant one, three, or five trees. An odd number is always recommended, since it's very difficult to achieve proper balance with an even number of elements *This preference for odd numbered elements runs throughout Japanese aesthetics.* The size of the trees depends a great deal on the size of the stone, but if large trees are chosen it is better not to use too many. When planting, always keep the visual movement of the rock in mind. All rocks have a feeling of motion, a direction in which the edges and peaks, from the base to the highest point, seem to be moving. If the rock has a focal point, such as a large cavity, that too must be considered.

Apply moss for visual effect and to help keep the soil in place.

Decide where the first tree should go.

Try to get all the roots you can into the pocket in the rock. Cut off any that stick out.

Secure the trees with wire and cover their roots with soil.

Adding a companion plant is a nice touch. Here a dwarf quince is used.

After all the trees are in place, make sure their roots are completely covered with soil.

Moisten flattened pieces of moss.

Scrape off as much soil as possible, so the moss will root well.

Then place the moss over the soil to prevent erosion.

POST-PLANTING CARE

There is no need for elaborate watering routines, provided the trees are not allowed to dry out completely. A couple of deep sprayings daily should suffice. *Because of the relatively small amounts of soil, you must watch for drying out. This is why the author recommends deep spraying twice a day. Be sure to spray the foliage when you spray the soil. If the rock is absorbent, spray the entire rock. Otherwise the rock will pull water out of the soil.*

Ten to fifteen days after planting is an ideal time to fertilize. *We recommend fish or other slow-release organic fertilizers, though any balanced fertilizer will do.*

If you live in a cold climate, the trees must be protected in winter. Just make sure they stay cool enough to avoid premature budding. If the rock is kept inside a shelter, inspect the moss carefully. If it withers and browns, the soil is too dry.

SHAPING

If you plant in the spring, by the fall the roots will have developed enough to allow you to begin shaping the trees. If you plant in early fall, you can start shaping the following spring, just before budding.

The first time you shape your *Zuishos*, identify the first and second branches and focus on those and the trunk, while allowing the rest of the tree to grow freely without pruning or wiring. Later, after the trunk has thickened a little, shaping will consist of wiring the entire tree, from the trunk to the last tiny branch. Do this once a year for three years. If you do this properly, you can perfectly balance the line of the trunk and the branches. After that, wiring roughly every five years should be enough.

Zuishos grow fast, so it's important not to decide too soon which of the branches will become the apex. In time it will become clear.

Normally, with five-needle pines, small branches at the base of main branches (*sacrifice branches*) are allowed to grow in order to thicken the main branches. However, with *Zuishos*, if you don't remove these little branches, they will quickly make the main branches too thick.

Seven months after planting, just before the first trimming and wiring. Height 24 inches (61 cm).

Two years after planting. The trees have matured considerably, but are still not completely rooted to the rock.

After the first trimming and wiring.

After the second trimming and wiring.

The primary tree before styling.

After.

The composition should form a scalene triangle. *No two sides or angles are the same on a scalene triangle. Compositions arranged in scalene triangles tend to appear both natural and harmonious.*

Four years after planting.

Rear view.

Long-term objective. The primary tree will be largest. Its foliage should make up half the total foliage mass, while the second and third trees will make up 30% and 20% respectively.

LONG-TERM TRAINING

Even when pinching back is done correctly, the tree will continue to grow. The only way to keep the trees in proper proportion to the rock is to prune radically every ten years or so.

It may even be necessary to cut the trunk down to the height of the third principal branch and begin creating a new tree from there. This may seem extreme, but with the *Zuisho's* rapid growth, it will be difficult to find even a trace of the scar in a few years.

ROCK SELECTION BASICS

Choosing the right stone is very important. Look for a stone that is powerful, with interesting character and texture. The stone is a miniature mountain, meant to stimulate the imagination of the viewer.

Just like bonsai, all stones have a front; study the stone from all directions to determine the best orientation. Look for stones that are hard; soft stones will tend to crumble with time. Avoid stones that are light in color (*darker stones tend to look older and more natural*). Finally, avoid stones that are too large to handle easily.

Stability is something you must consider when picking a stone. If you find an otherwise good stone that isn't stable, you can try chipping away part of the base or using a diamond-tipped saw blade to cut away part of the stone. An alternative is to use small stones as feet, affixing them with epoxy putty. Be sure to pick small stones that look like the larger stone. If you try this technique, you might want to experiment with various ways to conceal the joints of the feet. You can use ink or stone dust mixed into the epoxy, or apply a layer of auto body filler and color it, or cover visible joints with clear glue and press moss and lichen in place.

If you can't find a suitably dramatic stone, then consider joining several stones of similar color and texture, using the techniques described above. A collecting trip will often yield several stones which can be pieced together. Joining several stones together to create a larger one is an enjoyable project for the winter when your bonsai are at rest.

Jewel to Whirlpool

TRANSFORMING A FAMOUS OLD TREE

Artist: Tomio Yamada

This chapter illustrates the value of identifying and enhancing a tree's most distinctive features. Sometimes inexperienced enthusiasts will remove or hide something that has taken nature decades to develop, because it doesn't fit with their idea of what a bonsai should be. Often features that, at first glance, may appear eccentric or even ugly, are the very things that tell the true story of a tree.

This five-needle pine, *Pinus parviflora*, is thought to be more than 600 years old. It comes from the region around the river Hilo in Japan. It was originally named Jewel, for the circle in the center of the large *shari* on the trunk.

In June of 1955, a photograph (see below) of this distinguished old tree was first published in the *Shanshu-Do* book. The jewel was the main object of interest on the tree, demonstrated by the fact that the branches direct your gaze towards that area of the trunk.

In 1969 Jewel was shown at the *Shinjuku Bonsai and Suiseki Exhibition* (Shinjuku is a district in Tokyo) by the President of Japan, Shigueru Yoshida. In this photo, the *jewel-shari* appears less noticeable and less important.

If you compare the photographs (below), you'll notice that in 1955 the tree had a slanting motion, while in the 1969 photo, it was more vertical. Also, in the 1969 photo, the jewel is in the lower third of the trunk rather than midway as before.

In 1984, this masterpiece was shown in the magazine ***Kindai Bonsai*** (*Modern Bonsai*). This time the change was more radical. While the previous movement of the branches was primarily to the left, now they moved more to the right. This was achieved by removing the first branch on the left while allowing the first branch on the right to grow freely for a while and then lowering it. The 1984 trunk is also inclined more to the right.

On August 27, 1988, I began the restyling, anticipating the challenge of working on a tree already shaped several times by other artists. Each time I contemplated photos of its past, it seemed that the first person who designed the tree made the foliage dominate the tree's fine natural deadwood. No matter how I tried to understand the logic, it seemed senseless to use branches and foliage to hide more than 600 years of living history.

1955

1969

1984

It is never my intention to eliminate the influence of previous artists. Those long years of development, guided and shaped by others, can't simply be ignored or forgotten. When artists decide on certain characteristics, they have their reasons for doing so. If you decide to work with material that someone else has developed, you must carefully consider the thinking that motivated the original work.

I am still convinced that the most important thing about this tree is its jewel. Reshaping this deadwood gives me the idea that the name must be reflected in the design.

You'll notice that the *shari* continues around the trunk to the back. We will continue working and exposing the *shari* , following it to a *jin* on the left. Now, you can see why we need to change the name, as the *shari* has transformed from a *Jewel* to a *Whirlpool*.

The next step involves the branches. Notice how the foliage mass dominates the design and is very dense. We want to achieve a more open but no less dignified design. This will better harmonize the tree's shape and style with its age. It will also help show off its magnificent whirlpool.

Opening the tree without changing its position seems to be the best option. We begin by raising the first branch on the right, which droops in a cascading fashion. Then we'll prune the excessive foliage that hides the trunk. By exposing the lower part of the trunk, we add elegance as well as a little more visual height.

Jewel in 1987

The artist, Tomio Yamada at work.

The next step is to expose the bases of the major branches that are hidden by excessive foliage. Though at first glance you might think the tree has powerful branches fully covered with foliage, there is really a layer of foliage formed by many thin branches and a few thick branches. In order to rectify this problem, we need to emphasize the strong branches by removing almost all the small thin branches. This leaves the tree with half its original foliage, but there are still enough branches to ensure a mature and compact look. The pruning also allows more light and air inside the tree to stimulate new healthy buds. This will help revitalize the tree.

With very old trees you don't need to transplant very often, and in this case, we can wait another year. This will give the tree time to recover from all the pruning.

Now this grand old tree's new name, *Whirlpool*, is quite fitting.

Hosu, Jewel, before reshaping.
height 20" width 27" (51cm x 69cm)

The truly remarkable *shari* wrapping partway around the trunk...

...could not be seen from the front.

A hammer and chisel are used to start the new shari.

The new *shari* is taking shape.

1. Before expanding the shari.

2. After expanding the shari.

3. The new front.

4. After wiring the primary (right) branch.

5. After thinning the primary branch.

6. After shortening the first branch.

7. After thinning the left side and partially thinning the center and right side.

8. After finishing the thinning.

9. A close-up before much thinning was done.
(see #1 previous page)

10. A close-up after thinning.

THE RIGHT SIDE

Too many small branches obscure parts of the trunk and the bases of the larger branches.

THE BACK

After stripping the jin.

Before stripping the jin.

THE LEFT SIDE

Whirlpool, 1989, Height 19" (48cm). Before repotting. This will be the new front.

White Pine Gallery

Japanese white pine,
Pinus parviflora.
This rugged looking old tree was originally collected from the wild. The large shari on the right is what remains of a second trunk.
Height 30" (76 cm).

A perfect example of a literati (*bunjin*) clump-style on a ceramic slab. Japanese white pines commonly occur in clump style (*kabudachi*), as well as other styles that share a single root system. Height 28" (71 cm).

A Japanese white pine that has just been styled and repotted by Masahiko Kimura (1999). There's a stick pushing up a jinned branch and a piece of rebar in the back bracing the top of the tree until it sets into its new configuration. There are also several barely visible guy wires. Height 28" (72 cm).

Masahiko Kimura styled this multiple trunk (clump style) Japanese white pine together with this single piece of juniper deadwood in 1993. The deadwood doubles as a bonsai pot and a very dramatic shari. Height 29" (74 cm), width 40" (102 cm).

A literati (*bunjin*) Japanese white pine that has been planted on a stone. Rough-hewn, naturalistic pots are commonly used with literati style trees. Height 32" (81 cm).

This soulful old white pine, with its wild shari, hollowed-out trunk and aged bark is one of the most distinctive trees anywhere. It is quite famous in Japan and its picture often shows up in books, magazines and calendars. Height 29" (74 cm). Trunk diameter 10" (25 cm).

Kimura split three trunks into seven to create this distinctive literati-clump style white pine (see Bonsai Today 43). The trunks are all wrapped with raffia until the wounds heal. Approx. height 37" (94 cm).

A powerful informal upright white pine in a hand-etched Tokoname pot. Notice how the fluid curves of the trunk are exposed all the way up to the apex. Height 35" (89 cm), trunk diameter 10" (25 cm).

A slant style literati white pine in a handmade round pot. The heavy exposed root on the right and the long rightward moving branch across the upper trunk help counterbalance the strong lean to the left. Height 17" (43 cm).

This legendary formal upright Japanese white pine that was restyled by Kimura in 1997, is strongly reminiscent of the towering conifers in the western U.S. The straight trunk with its magnificent taper, as well as its superbly balanced branching and well-developed nebari, make it one of the few near perfect formal upright bonsai. Estimated height 42" (107 cm).

BLACK PINES

Japanese Black Pines

by Michael Persiano with Wayne Schoech

The power of this collected cork bark Japanese black pine is enhanced by its dark, deeply fissured bark.The strength of the surface roots conveys its stalwart character and capacity for holding its ground against the elements. From Japan, artist unknown.

OVERVIEW

Japanese black pines (*Pinus thunbergii*) have long been favorites of bonsai enthusiasts. Black pines, which thrive on oceanside cliffs, are very strong trees, capable of withstanding the challenges of natural elements and of human-altered environments. They are characterized by blackish trunks with heavily patterned bark and a network of strong branches and needles. The challenge with black pine bonsai is to express its strong character with bold and powerful designs.

As one of ten species classified as two-needle pines, *Pinus thunbergii*, the Japanese black pine, has numerous cultivars. Some of the most popular include: *Akame, Gan Sekki Sho, Hoko, Kotobuki, Kyokko, Nishiki, Yamaki* and various *Yatsubusa* (dwarf) varieties. This list is by no means comprehensive nor meant to discourage the use of other cultivars for bonsai.

The beautiful bark of the Japanese black pine can be seen in the photo above and in the photographic table (page 108), that compares trees grown in nature with those grown as bonsai. Notice the variety in the bark of the natural trees. While the length and diameter of the needles differ slightly from tree to tree, these differences are minor compared to the diversity of needles found on Japanese white pine cultivars.

Japanese black pines are not newcomers to Japanese gardening. This old, propped up specimen could easily double as a bonsai.

GENERAL INFORMATION

Needles Lustrous dark green. 2 per bundle, rigid, densely crowded, remaining for 2-3 years, 2-1/2″ to 4-1/2″ (6 to 11 cm) in nature and capable of being reduced to 1″ to 1-1/2" (2.5 to 4 cm) in bonsai.

Stem Color Lustrous green.

Bark The bark on immature trees becomes blackish gray while still quite young, and becomes fissured into elongated, irregular plates over time.

Growth Habit Generally uneven with pyramidal tendencies. In nature, older trees are characterized by spreading, pendulous branches. With aggressive pruning the natural growth easily develops density and conforms to most bonsai styles.

Size In nature, black pines range from 20-80′ (6-24 m) in height, with spreads of 20′ to 40′ (6-12 m). In bonsai, most trees range from 1′- 3′. 4′ is normally the maximum height for bonsai.

Hardiness Zones 4 or 5 to 8. In-ground trees survive temperatures as low as -15 Fahrenheit (-26 Celsius), although such exposure can result in damaged needles.

Growth Rate Medium, with the ability to easily achieve significant density over a 2-3 year period through aggressive feeding and energy balancing.

Culture Place your tree in full sun to insure health. Use fast-draining soils to protect against root-rot. Japanese black pines are remarkably salt-tolerant.

Common Diseases Needle Cast, Rust, Root Rot, Dieback, Tip Blight, and Canker.

Common Insects Sawflies, Scale, Needle Miner, Bark Beetles, and Shoot Borer.

South side.

North side.

Bark on in-ground black pines. Though there are some color variations, and other differences, note how the plate shapes are fairly constant.

Two views of a black pine bonsai with deeply fissured bark.

Two views of an old cork bark black pine bonsai.

Bark on some bonsai black pine varieties. Notice how much variation there is compared to the bark on the in-ground trees (top of page).

CARE AND MAINTENANCE

Candle Pinching, Bud Removal, Needle Plucking, and Pruning

Nothing is more critical to successfully growing Japanese black pines than mastering techniques for balancing energy. With all pine bonsai, candle pinching, bud removal, needle plucking, and pruning are the keys to developing well-balanced, horizontal growth and impressive designs.

Japanese black pines are more forgiving than Japanese white pines. They tolerate extremely hard cuts in the spring and bud profusely on 2 to 3 year-old wood, if fed aggressively and kept in direct sunlight.

SPRING CANDLE PINCHING

The following pinching method ***will not*** work for Japanese white pines. It is important to note that the timing used for candle pinching is based on the Mid-Atlantic region of the U.S. Be sure to make the necessary timing adjustments for other climates.

Before pinching back new candles (elongated buds), study your tree to identify the strong, medium, and weak growth zones, as indicated by the relative strength of the shoots. *Strong areas will have more abundant and healthier growth.*

From mid-April through May, use your thumb and index finger to pinch away 3/4 of the length of the candles in the strong zones.

In early June, remove all of the candles on branches in the medium strength zones, but ***do not*** remove any candles from the weak zones.

In late June or early July, return to the strong zones and completely remove all the new growth. Approximately 2-3 weeks later, new buds will appear. Carefully remove all but two of the new buds on each shoot. The removal of these buds marks the completion of your annual pinching activity.

If this is done properly, you will redirect energy from the strongest zone to the medium and weak zones. This should balance the energy in the entire tree. Eventually, when your tree is well balanced, this annual task will simplify to pinching candles back throughout the entire canopy to retain compact growth, and pruning back new shoots later in the growing season.

FALL NEEDLE PLUCKING

As with Japanese white pines, pulling old needles is essential; it allows light and air to penetrate and helps balance energy in the tree. Pull the old needle clusters (those closest to the trunk) very carefully to avoid tearing the bark. *Old needles are usually discolored and fairly easy to identify.*

From mid-October through mid-November, remove all of the previous year's needles in the strong and medium strength zones. Don't remove any of the old needles in the weakest areas. *They will eventually fall off on their own.*

From mid-November to early December, thin out the new needles in the strong zone, leaving 3-4 needle pairs per shoot. Perform this same task in the medium strength zone leaving 7-8 needle pairs per shoot. Don't remove any of the new needles in the weakest zone.

FALL PRUNING

Japanese black pines are pruned for aesthetic reasons and to promote budding. Unlike Japanese white pines, Japanese black pines tolerate hard pruning. This is a great asset when promoting back-budding. *Back-budding is when buds occur on old growth. Some trees back-bud easily, while others, most pines, included, don't.*

Prune away all unnecessary growth in the strong zone. This controls growth and diverts energy to the medium and weak zones. However, repeated and excessive hard pruning can be detrimental to the long term health of the tree. Allow your black pine to recover fully between hard prunings.

WINTER STORAGE

Unlike Japanese white pines, Japanese black pines have been successfully grown where the winters are quite mild. If you live in a warm area, you need not be concerned with this section.

When growing Japanese black pines where the winters are severe, protecting your trees is essential to their survival. There are several methods, but none of them are foolproof. Your choice should be tailored to the specific needs of your tree. Some of the popular methods for wintering Japanese black pine include cold frames, cold sheds, poly mini-houses, and cold garages. Whatever method you decide to use, air circulation is critical for the prevention of fungal disease and to deter insects. For more on winter protection see pages 18 & 19.

The following chapters provide an abundance of information on Japanese black pine styling, care, and maintenance from some of the most notable masters in the world. While their methods vary, their work ultimately achieves the same goal: outstanding trees.

Developing Short Needles

BALANCING GROWTH AND NEEDLE SIZE

This chapter is originally from Bonsai Today issue #2. The article is unattributed, so the artist will have to remain anonymous.

Many bonsai enthusiasts occupy themselves with the overall health of their trees, and don't pay enough attention to details like developing needles that are consistent with the size of the tree. This chapter explains the techniques used to reduce needle length on a Japanese black pine.

JAPANESE TERMS IN THIS SECTION

Yatsubusa – A variety exhibiting dwarfed characteristics. An example would be the 'Mikawa' Japanese black pine.

One of the main challenges in growing pines for bonsai is developing needles in proportion to the rest of the tree. There are two basic ways to accomplish this. The first is to use varieties which naturally have shorter needles and finer branching (*yatsubusa*). Or you can pinch and remove buds, candles, shoots and needles to increase the ramification (fine branching) of the tree and reduce the size of its needles. This chapter offers a needle reduction method that, although dedicated to the Japanese black pine, can be applied to any two-needle pine. We do not recommend using these techniques on three or five-needle pines.

You will sometimes hear the word proportion when speaking of leaf size. The notion of proportion as used in bonsai doesn't mean that the leaves or needles will be in the same relative scale as in full-size trees. In most cases this would be impossible. With bonsai, proper proportion simply means that the size of the leaves are small enough to harmonize with the overall size of the tree.

There are three distinct needle growth phases on a pine *(new vigorous needles, mature year-old needles, and two or three-year-old needles that are deteriorating and falling off)*. Pines are evergreens and this means that while they always have needles, they are not always from the same year. When some needles bud, others mature, and others fall.

If a branch has no needles, it will not bud. Therefore, you cannot totally defoliate a pine to reduce the size of its leaves as you would with some broad-leaved trees. Needle plucking must be gradual, with an understanding of the growth phase and the season. Needle plucking and selective bud removal balances the energy in all parts of the tree (*and reduces needle size*), encouraging the growth of the weakest buds by removing the strongest.

Generally, the most vigorous zones are the tips of the branches and the top of the tree, while the weakest are in the interior of the lower branches. The rest of the zones are usually of medium vitality. The following method may be stressful to your trees, so it is important that they are healthy and vigorous.

SHOOT PRUNING

SHOOT PRUNING

The sequence from bud to candle to shoot to branch is helpful to understand. When spring growth begins, buds that were developed the previous year become candles. Candles are tight cylindric elongated buds. Soon after the candles elongate, they open (the needles spread). After opening, they continue to elongate and become shoots. These shoots continue growing and eventually become full-fledged branches.

Shoot pruning is generally undertaken in early summer when spring buds have matured into shoots. Begin first by pinching or cutting *(if the shoots have begun to harden, you might find cutting easier than pinching)* the weak shoots (leave 1/16″ stub) and then, about ten days later, the stronger ones. At the same time that you cut the weak shoots, you can pull the new needles on the strong shoots, leaving only their sheaths. This sequence encourages the weaker shoots to put forth new secondary buds before the stronger shoots do. If a shoot is very weak, it is better not to touch it until it is as strong as the rest of the shoots in the vicinity.

BUD REMOVAL

About two weeks after pinching, a new second growth will begin to appear in the fascicles of the needles, just below where the weak shoots were removed. This is the time to remove the stripped sections of the strong shoots. *As with the weak shoots, leave a stub about 1/16″ long.*

Later, selectively remove some of the new secondary buds, as the diagrams show. On weak shoots, remove the weak new buds and leave the strongest ones. On stronger shoots, remove the strongest new buds and leave the weaker ones. This balances the budding in all parts of the tree, allowing the energy from the roots to be shared more equitably.

NEEDLE THINNING

By October the budding is finished. If you are lucky, all the buds will now be about the same size. The old needles will begin to take on a yellow or reddish color and some will fall off. Now it is time to eliminate the remaining old needles (*those previously left at the base of the pinched shoots*) with tweezers. This will allow more sunlight and air to reach inside the tree.

In late December or early January, remove some of the new needles. In strong areas, leave only 3 or 4 pairs per shoot. In weak areas, leave 5 or 6 pairs. Again, don't touch the needles on the very weakest shoots. This will give them a chance to catch up with the others.

TRIMMING SECOND GROWTH BUDS

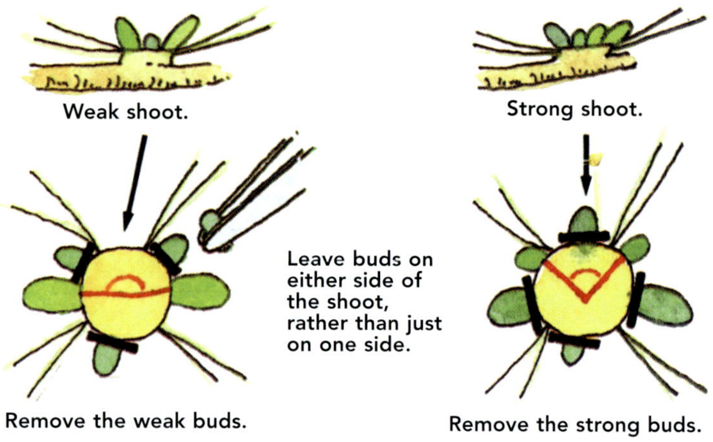

NEEDLE THINNING

A REAL LIFE EXAMPLE

Now let's apply our needle reduction procedures to a real example: a Japanese black pine that was grown in the ground for two years and then put in a training pot for a year, and prepared for needle reduction by heavy fertilizing. *A generous feeding program ensures vigorous bud growth.*

As you can see, this pine has both strong and weak areas and most of the needles are too long for the size of the tree. If the tree was not healthy, or if we had transplanted it this year, simply pruning the apex would avoid excessive stress and would be a better approach. In this case, the tree is quite strong, so we can confidently embark on a full needle reduction sequence.

LATE JUNE 1984

First, cut the shoots in the weak zones with very sharp scissors. Remember, extremely weak shoots should not be touched. Again, cut about 1/16" above the old needles. Then, using tweezers, remove the new needles from the sheaths of the strongest shoots.

ABOUT TEN DAYS LATER

The buds in the weak region are beginning to grow. Now cut the shoots in the strong zones about 1/16" above the old needles.

LATE JULY 1984

A month after pinching, the new buds have elongated considerably *(these elongated buds are called candles)* and some are even at the point of opening. This is the time to selectively remove them, eliminating weak buds (*or candles*) from the weak zones and strong buds from the strong growth zones. You can do this with your fingers, but using tweezers helps avoid damaging the remaining buds. Leave 2 buds in stronger areas and 3 or 4 buds in weaker areas.

EARLY OCTOBER 1984

In October remove last year's needles, except on sparse branches which need more buds. The following spring, candle or shoot pinching on these sparse branches will encourage the formation of adventitious buds among the old needles in the newly lignified *(woody)* areas. *This process of forcing new buds on the lower parts of branches is called back-budding. Many plants easily form back-buds. With black pines, back-budding isn't guaranteed, but can be accomplished on healthy, vigorously growing trees. Proper care and especially generous feeding is the key to successful back-budding.*

This pine was started from seed three years ago. For the first two years it was grown in the ground (field grown) to thicken the trunk. In its third spring, it was put into this training pot and fertilized with a high nitrogen fertilizer every two weeks. Height 10" (25 cm).

A close-up of a weak zone.

A medium zone. The top of the tree (see top photo), with its vigorous candles, is the strong zone.

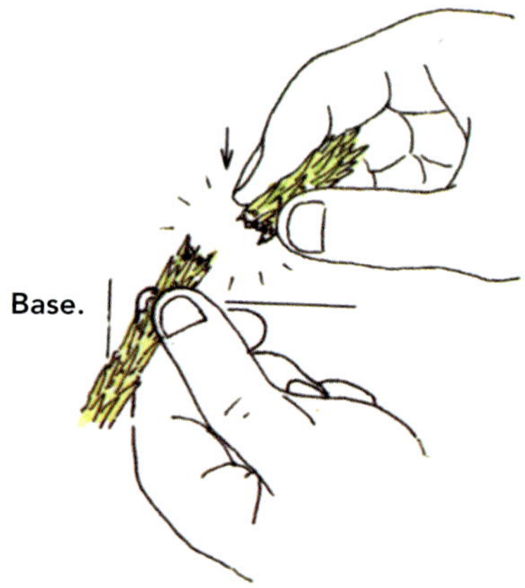

Do this by hand in order not to damage future needles.

What was a bud in July is now a little branch.

You can shorten the shoots on the apex ...

... or you can simply remove the apex.

MID-WINTER 1984-85

You should leave pruning the apex until midwinter, because the tree will feel the effects less when it's dormant. When pruning the apex, you need to distinguish weak and strong branches. On strong branches *(most of the apex will be strong, but some parts will be stronger than others)*, remove the strong shoots, and on weak branches that you want to strengthen, remove the weak shoots.

If you are not ready to radically reduce the apex, you'll need to at least shorten the shoots when they extend in the spring. This will stimulate the growth of lower buds. However, the tree's energy will be more balanced if you actually remove the apex. *On this tree, the design objective involves greatly reducing the height of the tree by removing its current apex. Obviously, this doesn't mean that you need to remove the apex on just any tree.*

MID-APRIL 1985

The buds are beginning to swell and will soon elongate. The photograph shows two zones marked with blue. All the buds on the apex are the same size. All the buds on the lower branches are also the same size. However, if we compare the two zones, the buds on the apex are stronger than those on the lower branches.

To correct this imbalance, use your thumb and index finger to pinch away 3/4 of the length of each candle in the strong zone. In the weak zone, just let the candles grow.

MID-JULY 1985

The tree's growth has corrected itself considerably, but the shoots at the apex are still too vigorous *(the candles have opened and are now new shoots)*. Now you will need scissors, as the shoots are beginning to harden. Cut the longest ones off just below the new needles. Cut the medium shoots halfway between the base and the new needles. Remove the weakest shoots.

MID-AUGUST 1985

The secondary buds are beginning to grow from amongst the old needles. When they are approximately 1/4″ long, it's time to remove the unwanted ones. Keep only those that are growing in desirable directions. In the photographs, we eliminated most of the old needles before their time, so you can see the new buds. Normally you would leave the old needles until October.

After removing the old apex and thinning the new one.

Where to prune.

There are too many buds in this strong area.....

In these two photos, needles were removed so you can clearly see the buds.

.... leave only the ones growing in desirable directions.

There are too many buds growing at the end of this strong branch.......

.... remove all but two or three.

When the buds are about 1/4 inch long remove the ones that grow in the wrong direction.

In this weak area in the middle of the tree.....

... leave six or seven buds on each branch.

Warning: We have removed more needles than usual so you can see the new buds. Though this tree is doing quite well, such drastic needle reduction is unnecessary and potentially dangerous.

JULY 1986

Two years later. The tree has changed considerably. Healthy and strong, it was transplanted in the early spring into a bonsai container. From now on, selectively remove unwanted buds only every two or three years. Pinching and needle removal should be done every year.

After transplanting the shoots were allowed to grow for awhile so the tree could regain its strength.

Late August 1986. After wiring and pruning. You will still need to pinch the apex regularly to keep it under control.

From the top.

The future

SUMMARY:

Reducing needle size, as well as creating a harmonious overall design requires balancing the flow of energy. Before initiating any work on your tree, it is important to identify strong and weak zones.

No one method is the definitive approach to balancing energy. Explore various approaches and determine which works best for you.

No matter which methods you use, it is important to apply balancing techniques annually. Neglect will result in gangly overgrown trees with long needles.

The variety of approaches to balancing growth is a testament to the resilience of the Japanese black pine.

Your ultimate goal with these rather complex techniques is energy balancing. Over the years, we have encountered numerous energy balancing methods. Though all are somewhat similar, some are quite complex and some relatively simple. No matter which method you choose, don't be afraid to work on your Japanese black pine. In the universe of trees, it is one of the most forgiving varieties. Feel free to experiment and learn as you go. Ultimately, you will arrive at a workable energy balancing solution.

After thinning the apex

After needle pulling

After pruning and wiring

Creating a Cascade

STYLING, BALANCING & REDUCING NEEDLE SIZE *Artist: Oishi Kasan*

A classic cascade style Japanese black pine with companion.

Have you noticed how few good cascade bonsai there are? There's a good reason for this shortage; cascade bonsai present unique challenges, not the least of which is the fact that most plants don't naturally grow downward. Black pines are no exception. Like most trees they are apically dominant, so getting energy to flow down to support lower growth can be quite challenging. This is where energy balancing and other skills come in. In spades. Though energy balancing is a must with any black pine bonsai, with cascades, it is doubly important.

THE CASCADE MYSTIQUE

Imagine a tree growing on a precipice with the sea crashing below. Cascade bonsai capture the drama of this scene; the strength of the trunk bowing toward the void, enduring harsh winds and violent storms.

Cascade bonsai can assume myriad forms. The trick, no matter what the form, is finding a way to keep the cascading branches and the apex in balance.

In this chapter we follow twelve years in the development of a cascading black pine. Our primary focus is to explore the methods used to evenly distribute the vigor of the tree.

CASCADE BASICS

1. Plan the shape of the trunk and the primary cascading branch carefully. All other branches are of secondary importance. The cascading branch is the main feature on a cascade style tree. No other feature takes precedence in the composition.

2. If the nebari is good (*if the exposed surface roots are well balanced*), so much the better, but nebari is not as important with cascade bonsai as with other styles. With upright styles, the trunk is the main feature, so how the nebari visually supports the trunk is very important. With cascades, the cascading branch is the main feature and the trunk, though still important, is secondary.

3. If possible, the heaviest exposed roots should grow opposite the cascading branch. Because of the strong visual weight of the cascading section, it is desirable to have a strong surface root on the opposite side of the trunk. This creates counterbalance and stability, and a sense of connection to the earth.

An excellent nebari; strong on the side opposite the cascading branch.

4. Be careful not to let the apex dominate the design. The upper section of a cascading tree should be balanced with the cascading section. Because energy will naturally flow toward the apex, you must exercise careful control over bud development and other energy balancing techniques, or you'll end up with an unbalanced tree.

5. Flexibility in the shape and position of the cascading branch is okay. In some cases it can even fall toward the front. The cascading branch is the factor around which the tree is organized (*just like the trunk in upright bonsai*). Its position can move forward or to either side, depending on the nature of the tree and your preference. In many cases, you have more flexibility in positioning a cascading branch than you do with primary branches on upright trees.

6. The secondary branches growing off the main cascading branch should be horizontal. Just like branches that grow off an upright trunk, branches grow horizontally off the main cascading branch. The difference is, with upright bonsai, the branches usually grow out and slightly down, away from the upward movement of the trunk, while the branches on a cascading bonsai grow out and slightly down, toward the downward movement of the cascading branch. This is because of gravity and snow load. With bonsai we want to create the illusion of age, and in nature, old branches tend to sag.

CULTIVATION: THE BEGINNING

Cascade bonsai magnify the tendency of lower branches to be weaker than upper branches. In two-line cascades (*apex plus cascade*), this difference can significantly weaken the cascading branch, unless you do something to correct the imbalance.

Creating a cascade style begins with the branch that will become the cascade. This branch should be established before the upper section. If the process is reversed, the top section will rob most of the energy from the cascading section.

When starting from seed, let the future cascading branch grow up and out, until it is quite long. Once the trunk has thickened, prune and wire the branch into a cascading form. After you've styled the tree, needle plucking and bud pinching are crucial. To do this properly, you must consider the vitality of three general areas: those of great vigor, those of medium strength, and those that are weak.

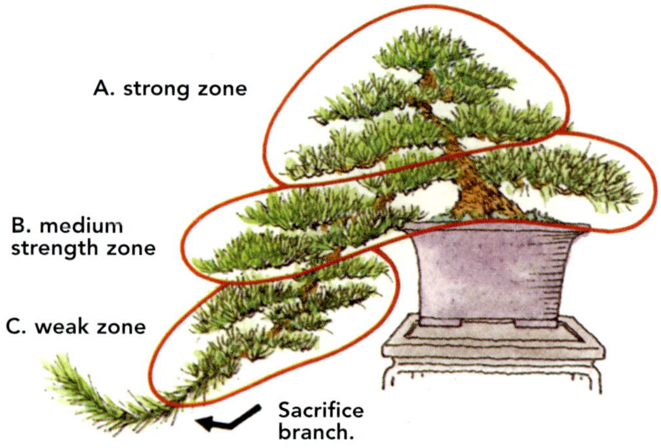

CANDLE PRUNING

If you do it early when the candles are still soft, you can pinch them with your fingers.

If the candles are too weak in zone C, don't touch them. Just remove the strong candles in zone B. One week later, do the same in zone A.

If you do remove candles in zone C, do them first. Then one week later do zone B and one week after that do zone A.

NEEDLE THINNING

Zone A: on younger trees, leave 4 or 5 new needles per shoot

Zone A: on mature trees, leave only 3 needles per shoot.

Zone B: leave 7 or 8 new needles per shoot

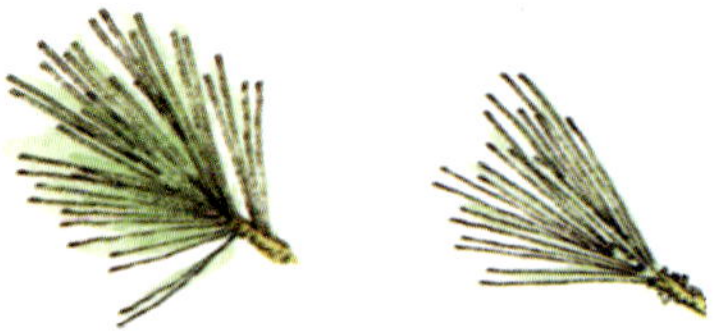

Zone C: leave all the new needles

CANDLE PINCHING

The best time to pinch candles (*candles are simply elongated buds*) is over a two-week period in early summer. Before starting, determine the strongest, medium, and weakest zones. It is important to note that the weakest candles in all three zones should be allowed to grow and should not be pinched back. The first step is to eliminate the strongest candles (*if any*) in the weakest zone (C). Approximately one week later, remove all the candles (*except the very weak ones*) in the medium zone (B). After another week, remove all the candles (*except the very weak ones*) in the strongest zone (A). This simple procedure will go a long way toward balancing the vigor of your black pine bonsai.

NEEDLE THINNING

Needles are thinned from fall to early spring, just before transplanting time. Thinning needles regulates the amount of photosynthetic energy produced. The greater the number of needles, the greater the energy produced in that area.

Be careful removing needles, especially if it is intensely cold. If you remove too many, the remaining needles may weaken and die. If this happens, you can lose whole branches. This also applies to pruning. Pruning creates stress. It is possible to prune too much in a area, weakening or killing branches, or even whole trees.

Carefully pull out the old needles and some of the new ones in the strongest areas, leaving four or five pairs of new needles per shoot. Use tweezers if necessary. In medium strength areas, remove old needles and leave seven or eight pairs of new needles. In the weak areas, remove only the old needles. If the branch or shoot is especially weak, don't touch any needles. Leave even the old ones.

1977 TO 1980

The tree has been allowed to grow freely

The original apex has been wired down to form the cascading branch

1974-1982; THE EARLY YEARS

This black pine was originally collected from nature in 1974. The nebari was quite good and the trunk had pleasant curves and a good taper. However, the crown was completely undeveloped, consisting of only one long, young branch and a weak secondary shoot growing opposite the trunk's incline.

Generally, the growth of the apex should be controlled on a regular basis. But in this case, since the apex is being developed from a small lateral shoot, that control is unnecessary. *At least for now. Later, when the apex has developed, regular control will be necessary.*

During the first few years, both branches are left to grow freely, with slight pruning at the tip of the longest one to encourage the growth of the smaller one. After three years, ramification (*branching*) begins. Now the branch that will become the apex is cut back to begin an ongoing process of transferring energy to the cascading branch. Then both branches are wired. They are then positioned at the desired angle and shaped to add curves, avoiding the monotony of straight lines. *When shaping with wire, add movement in both dimensions; front to back and side to side.*

ADDING MOVEMENT TO PRIMARY BRANCHES

Master Kasan brings up an important question: when is the best time to introduce movement to primary branches? With this tree, movement is introduced early on, while the branches are still supple. If we wait too long, extensive measures will be required. *Though it is a bit more difficult, the right tools, properly used, allow bending of large branches with minimal risk. See pages 155, 160 & 161 for details.*

FERTILIZING

In the early years, heavy use of high-nitrogen fertilizer produces abundant growth. Secondary shoots appear everywhere and rapidly become secondary and tertiary branches. *Japanese black pines are quite responsive to high-nitrogen fertilizer. For information on intensive feeding see page 36.*

Winter 1980. After one year of pinching and pruning, secondary branches are forming.

Winter 1982. The tree has been moved to a larger pot to hasten development. The cascading branch is quite strong; time to remove the sacrifice branch.

Sacrifice branch. Cut to just below a needle cluster that is pointing in the direction you want the new growth to go. (In this illustration you cut just above the needles cluster. With a cascading branch you cut just below the cluster.)

WINTER 1982

From 1980 to 1982, Master Kasan applies candle pruning and needle thinning techniques, except on the apex and the sacrifice branch. Although he prunes the sacrifice branch twice to redirect energy to upper shoots, he doesn't pinch the candles or thin the needles. Why bother when the sacrifice branch will soon be removed?

Sacrifice branches are used to thicken sections of trunk or branches, or to strengthen specific areas. For thickening, allow one or more sacrifice branches to grow unimpeded immediately above the area to be thickened. Unimpeded growth creates an accelerated flow of sap, while pruning slows down the flow. For example, if you want to thicken a trunk's base while slowing its growth above the base, you encourage a sacrifice branch a few inches up the trunk, while trimming to inhibit growth in the areas above the sacrifice branch.

When you do this, much of the tree's energy flows into the unimpeded sacrifice branch, passing through the lower trunk on its way. As energy flows through an area (in this case the base of the trunk), nutrients that cause thickening are deposited. When the desired thickness has been reached, the sacrifice branch is removed (sacrificed).

If an area loses strength, develops weakened buds, or fails to produce fruit or flowers (this usually occurs in the lower sections of a tree), let the branches in that area grow freely for awhile. This free growth slowly pulls more energy through the weak areas, and should eventually correct the problem.

In most cases, using a sacrifice branch to thicken the main branch or the trunk is desirable. However, in this case Master Kasan keeps his eye on the situation to make sure that the strong cascading branch doesn't inhibit the growth of the apex. *Usually it is the other way around; the apex inhibits the growth of the cascading branch.*

April 1986. Notice how the needles are longer on the right side of the apex. That's because it is being treated as the weak area. Later the process will reverse and the cascade branch will be treated as the weak area.

October 1986. Now the strength is equalized and we can concentrate on refinement. Notice how all the branches have been cleaned up and made visible. Removing hanging twigs and needles to expose branches is an important bonsai technique that is often overlooked.

FEBRUARY 1985

When the sacrifice branch on the cascade is eliminated, it becomes clear that Master Kasan's concerns are justified. From 1983 to 1985, the sacrifice branch worked too well. The result is too much strength in the cascading branch and not enough in the apex.

This is not only because of the sacrifice branch. From the beginning, there was a pronounced difference in strength between the strong branch that is now the cascade, and the small shoot that is now the apex.

APRIL 1985 AND OCTOBER 1986

Now comes the refinement stage. It's time to reverse the normal process and compensate for the imbalance. For the following round of candle pinching and needle thinning, Master Kasan treats the apex as a weak area, and the cascade as an area of medium strength.

Compare the photographs taken in 1985 and 1986. Appreciable changes are easily observed not only in the apex, but throughout the tree. Because no area was treated as a strong area, the entire tree developed abundant healthy foliage.

As you've seen, by 1985 the treatment of the candles and needles has caused the foliage to grow excessively dense. If you maintain that much foliage for too long, it deprives the interior of light and air, and destroys small buds that would normally become future branches. Though he has already done some reduction, if Mr. Kasan waits too much longer to start seriously reducing foliage mass, it will be impossible to maintain the health of the interior of the tree.

In the 1986 photo, some small branches have been removed from the apex and a small shoot has been wired up to create a new apex. Opposite branches were removed and the remaining branches were cleaned up to allow more air and light into the interior. Even after all this effort, the foliage is still quite dense.

In refining the tree, Master Kasan has tried to separate masses of foliage. This adds depth and creates open space for visual contrast. In the future, a diligent combination of pruning, thinning and wiring, will ensure that this powerful cascade pine will become even more majestic and dramatic than it already is.

SUMMARY

1. In cascade style, no other branch takes precedence over the cascading branch.

2. Secondary branches are positioned horizontally along the primary cascading branch.

3. If there is an upper crown in the design, it should not be dominant. If the crown is too strong, it will weaken the cascading branch. A dominant crown can also visually overpower the cascading branch (crown and apex are often used interchangeably. However, sometimes apex will refer to just the branch at the tip of a tree, and crown will refer to the whole top section of a tree.)

4. Cascading branches can fall towards the viewer or to either side. In this respect, the guidelines are looser than with branches in other styles. The basic rule is: follow your instincts and position the cascade in a way that enhances the inherent beauty of the tree.

The scar from the sacrifice branch. Notice how the needle cluster that was left just above the cut has become a small branch that hides the scar.

1985. Notice how well ramified the crown has become in a few short years.

1986. The crown after candle pruning and needle thinning.

October 1986. Though the tree now has good overall balance, there are still some branches that are stronger than others. Here you can compare two secondary branches. The upper branch is quite strong and shows excellent ramification, while the lower weaker branch has poor ramification. Ramification is simply branching. In these cases, secondary branching growing off primary branches.

These two photos show the cascading branch from the top and bottom. Notice how well developed the secondary and tertiary branches are and how their ends form desirable triangular shapes. This intricate branch development is one of the things that distinguishes the pro from the dilettante.

October 1986. Height, from the bottom of the pot to the tip of the apex, 27 inches. Diagonal length, from the tip of the apex to the tip of the cascading branch, 35 inches.

Unfortunately, we never received a finished photo of the tree cleaned up and ready for exhibition. Even so, you can get a pretty good idea of the tree's future from the photos we have.

Choosing a Pot

THAT ACCENTUATES A TREE'S BEST FEATURES

Author unknown. This chapter was unattributed when it originally appeared in Bonsai Today issue 18.

The challenge in this short chapter is to select a quality pot that harmonizes with, and enhances a tree's unique character. We sometimes forget that a bonsai is both a tree and a pot. Just as a poorly chosen pot can cheapen a tree, a well chosen pot can elevate it.

Before reading the captions under each photo, try to select the best pot for the tree. While there is no absolute answer, there is usually a single pot that works best for any given tree.

Japanese terms in this section: Nebari – Surface roots Tachiagari – Lower trunk

1. Japanese black pine, *Pinus thunbergii*. Height 30". Pot dimensions: 18" high by 9" wide (46 x 23 cm).

2. The height seems right, but there is too much decoration.

3. Too stylized for such a full crown.

4. Too ornate.

5. Too similar to original.

6. Too big.

7. Too small.

8. This one is just right.

CHOOSING A POT FOR AN OLD BLACK PINE

The Japanese black pine in this chapter was trained in the semi-cascade style. Pot selection is complicated for two reasons: the trunk and the cascading branch are very dynamic, while the crown is heavy and more static.

The dense crown is suited to a heavy, rounded pot that is not too tall. The cascade, however, calls for a lighter pot that doesn't overpower it and that complements the line of the trunk.

Of course, you could always resort to a standard cascade pot, as shown in photos 2 and 3. However, neither of these are quite right. Now take a look at all the photos. Which would you choose? After several tries and near misses, we settled on number 8 — an elegant round pot that is narrower at the base than at the rim. *An added touch is the raised horizontal band which enhances the line of the cascading branch.*

After selecting the pot, the design of the tree needs changing. Lightening the heavy crown by opening up spaces between the branches makes the movement of the trunk more visible.

It is not unusual for a pot to prompt us to alter a tree. In this case, because the pot is relatively small and light, the weight of the tree needs to be reduced, otherwise it will overpower the pot. At least two things are accomplished by opening up the crown — the mass of the tree is reduced to harmonize with the pot, and the powerful dynamic trunk is exposed.

Pot color is another issue worth discussing. With pines and other conifers, unglazed pots are preferred. Subdued gray and brown pots provide a nice contrast to lush, verdant pine needles. These colors also tend to harmonize with the colors of pine bark. Generally, glazed or colored pots are not used with pines — the color tends to draw your attention away from the tree. Flowering varieties or varieties with striking or colorful leaves are better suited to colored pots.

It is a good idea to have several suitable pots on hand before you start transplanting. If you can afford to do this, you will be able to change your selection as the transplanting process unfolds. Often the pot we choose before we start isn't the pot we end up using.

Transplanting
& NEBARI DEVELOPMENT

Some of this chapter is unattributed material from Bonsai Today issue 17. The rest was written by Wayne Schoech.

In order to discuss nebari development, we need to discuss transplanting – each time you transplant is an opportunity to work on the nebari.

Transplanting black and white pines is not that much different than transplanting most other bonsai. Though some things are specific to pines, most general guidelines for transplanting should be followed.

As far as the difference between black and white pines goes, when it comes to transplanting – well, there really isn't much. Because most white pines are grafted onto black pine stock, the roots are the same for both varieties. Ungrafted white pines obviously have roots that are different from black pines, but when it comes to transplanting, the differences are minor.

WHEN AND HOW OFTEN DO YOU TRANSPLANT?

Early spring, when the new buds are just beginning to swell, is the best time to transplant. However, you can transplant black pines (or white pines on black pine rootstock) in the late summer, though you don't want to do heavy rootpruning then unless you live somewhere with very mild winters. Better to stick to spring transplanting with white pines growing on their own roots.

How often you need to transplant will depend upon the length of your growing season, how much you fertilize, and other factors. With mature pines, every three to five years is typical. Young trees that are still vigorously growing need to be transplanted more often.

CHOOSING A POT

Before you start, you need a pot. Actually, it is good to have several pots to choose from, if you can afford this luxury. Sometimes the pot you think is best before you start isn't the best by the time you finish.

Traditionally, pines and other conifers are planted in unglazed brown or grey pots. Their subdued earthy tones go well with rugged pine bark and lush needles. Colored pots work better with trees that have flowers or colorful foliage. As far as shape goes, this is determined more by the characteristics of the individual tree than by the species.

SOIL

For pines and other conifers, akadama is the soil of choice for most enthusiasts and professionals. Though akadama comes from Japan, it is now available in the west. The only real problem is the price — if you want something more affordable, there are several good domestic mixes that are available through bonsai suppliers and nurseries. Be careful though; unless you know your source, you can't be sure how good the mix is. If you have questions, call a reputable supplier or check with a local bonsai club.

Akadama

If you use akadama, you'll have to decide upon particle hardness. Akadama comes in soft, medium and hard particles. In dry to moderately dry climates, most people use soft particles. In wet climates, most people use medium-hard particles. The hardest particles are seldom used, and are usually mixed with other ingredients.

No matter what soil you use, you need to make sure it's as clean as possible. Even soil that has already been screened should be screened again just before you transplant. For more on soil, see pages 14 & 15.

EXPOSING AND PROTECTING THE NEBARI

Let the soil dry out before you start. After you remove the tree from its old pot, gently scrape the top layer of soil off with a wooden or bamboo stick (don't use a metal tool). You want to avoid damaging the surface roots (nebari), so be careful. Start at the base of the trunk and gently scrape outward. Go all the way around the trunk, carefully scraping only from the trunk out, following the direction of the roots. Do this as many times as necessary to expose the surface roots. Be sure not to scrape laterally across the roots.

This Japanese white pine is ready to have its rootball taken apart.

This scraping serves primarily to remove old soil and expose the nebari — but it also helps to remove moss and other organic materials, as well as minerals, fertilizer and pesticide residue that have built up over time.

TAKING THE ROOTBALL APART

Don't cut the roots before taking the rootball apart. You need to see exactly what you have before you cut. Start by thumping your fist on the bottom of the rootball to dislodge loose soil. Then, starting at the bottom, use a stick and start removing soil and untangling roots. Don't use a steel roothook unless you have to. Working from the bottom up, open the rootball by combing outward (towards the side of the rootball) rather than downward. Work slowly and try not to damage the roots as you comb them out. You are finished with this stage when all the roots have been untangled and combed out.

REMOVING OLD SOIL

Most of the old soil will come off when you comb the roots out. There are two options for the soil that remains — you can remove all of it, or you can leave some just below the base of the trunk.

A pressurized stream of water and a wooden stick are the best way to remove old soil.

THE FIRST TRANSPLANTING

With fieldgrown trees, collected trees, or trees in nursery pots, it is important to get all of the old soil off, as it is usually quite different (much heavier in most cases) than bonsai soil and will cause drainage problems. With pines, you should take the old soil off in two stages — half with the first transplanting and half with the next. With deciduous and some other trees, you can take it off all at once.

When you decide to remove all the old soil, a pressurized stream of water works best. Use your wooden stick with the water to help dislodge tough old particles. If you have a particularly stubborn rootball, you can stick it in a tub of water and use your fingers to remove the soil and comb the roots out.

SUBSEQUENT TRANSPLANTINGS

When you transplant trees that are already in bonsai soil, you have at least two choices — if the tree is healthy, you can remove all of the old soil. If the tree is stressed, or the old soil is still good, you can leave some soil at the base of the trunk. If you do leave some soil, be sure to remove it the next time you transplant.

ROOTPRUNING AND DEVELOPING THE NEBARI

A good nebari consists of thick roots growing radially from all sides of the trunk. They should all emerge from the trunk at the same level (or close to the same level) and enter the soil gradually and smoothly, more or less the same distance from the trunk.

Nebari take time to develop — don't expect to find perfect surface roots the first time you transplant. However, by rootpruning and employing other techniques each time you transplant, you can have a top-notch nebari in a few years.

After cleaning off the old soil, the next step is rootpruning. First, remove all the roots that grow strongly downward. This encourages lateral growth and helps flatten the rootball.

Next, remove lateral roots with defects that can't be corrected, or that you don't otherwise need for the nebari. These can include roots that plunge abruptly into the soil, roots that grow out from the trunk at odd angles, roots on top of other roots, roots that are curled or otherwise misshapen, crossing roots, and sometimes even roots that are too thick relative to the other roots in the nebari. After you cut off a thick root, clean up the wound with a chisel and then apply cutpaste.

Sometimes there are just too many surface roots and and you may have to remove some that might otherwise be useful. In this case, keep the thickest and best situated.

All the downward growing roots have been removed.

Some people use two sticks to clean the nebari.

After cleaning off the soil, it's time to begin pruning the surface roots.

Root cutters and other biting tools work best.

Because it is often difficult to find perfect roots for a nebari, you may need to correct roots that appear defective. The best way to do this is to start when the tree is young and the roots are flexible and easy to shape and move. Some techniques for moving roots are: using a stone to separate two roots, anchoring a root (even more than one) to a stick for straightening, using a razor blade to separate roots that have fused together, and using a chisel to split a thick root into two.

Sometimes you need to move roots that are too high or too low. Though this is not always easy, and there are limits to how far you can move a root, there are techniques for doing this. An effective way to force roots down is to use flexible bamboo sticks (see photo). Sticks can also be used to move roots up. As with branches, wire can also be used to move roots.

As long as there are ingenious people around, there will be new ways to do things. Some clever ways to develop a nebari are shown below and on the following pages.

A freshly pruned nebari.

You can use a stick to raise roots you need for the nebari.

Use a chisel to clean large cuts and then seal with cutpaste.

You can use a chisel to create two smaller roots from one large root.

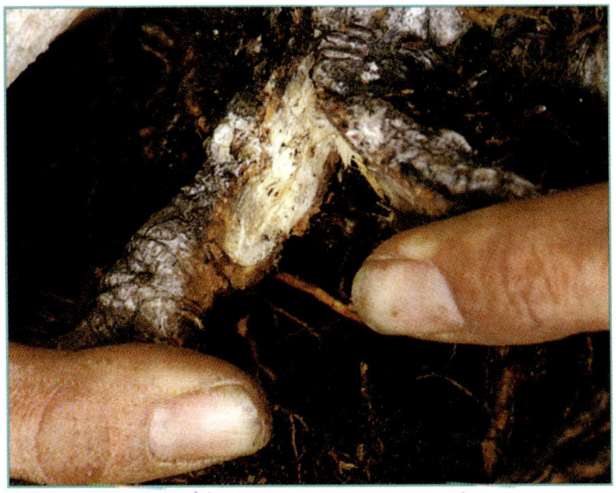

After using the chisel, you can separate the root using your fingers. Be careful not to damage the fine feeder roots.

You can use a stone to keep the two new roots apart.

Though this tree is not a pine, the technique still works for lowering surface roots. First, wire down some bamboo sticks. After you put in a bottom layer of soil, bend the sticks up one at a time and slide the roots underneath. The sticks will keep pressure on the roots, and gradually lower them to the right level.

Placing a slab of polystyrene in the middle of the pot promotes horizontal root growth and the development of a wider nebari.

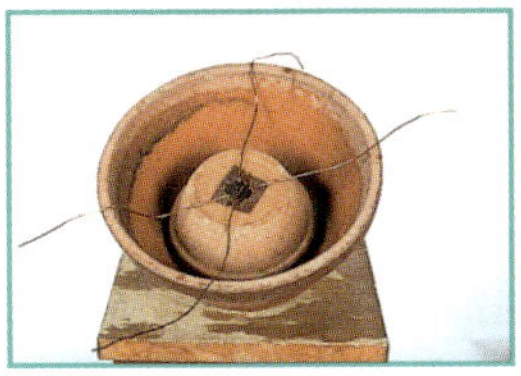

A little pot inside a big pot is another technique for developing a nebari. Once the screen and anchoring wire are set in the bigger pot, pass wire through the drainage hole of the smaller pot, and cover that hole with another piece of screen, to prevent soil from falling through. Spread the roots evenly over the small pot when you transplant.

ACCELERATED NEBARI DEVELOPMENT

1. PRUNE DOWNWARD GROWING ROOTS

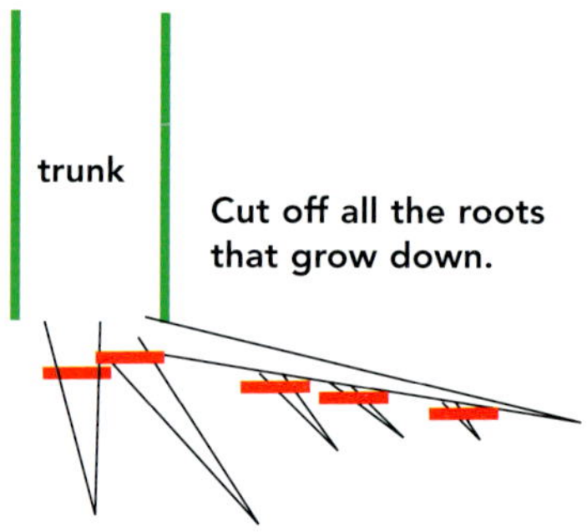

All root treatment during transplanting is based on this foundation. In the same way that branch shoots tend to grow upward, roots grow downward, guided by the force of gravity. If you want a wide nebari, that growth must be held in check by pruning all the roots growing down. Occasionally, some of the downward-growing roots are flexible enough to be moved into a horizontal position, making pruning unnecessary.

2. BALANCE THE STRENGTH OF THE ROOTS

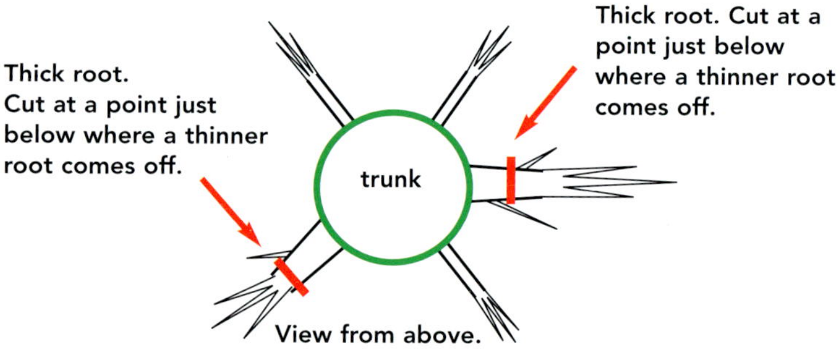

In bonsai, balance is basic. Not because it is simple, but because it is essential. It is the foundation upon which bonsai rests. Balancing the strength of the branches is an obvious priority, but don't forget the roots. It is essential to balance root growth.This will then be reflected in the strength of the nebari, trunk and branches. Prune as shown in the drawing, shortening the thick roots and letting the thinner ones grow. Eventually, all the roots will be the same length and blend into a wide nebari. Nebari is the Japanese word for the group of exposed surface roots that radiate out from the base of the trunk. A good nebari lends both a sense of balance and age to a bonsai. Sometimes the roots of a nebari will fuse together into a solid mass. This is most common with trident maples and certain other deciduous trees.

3. RE-ARRANGE THE SURFACE ROOTS SO THEY GROW AT THE SAME LEVEL

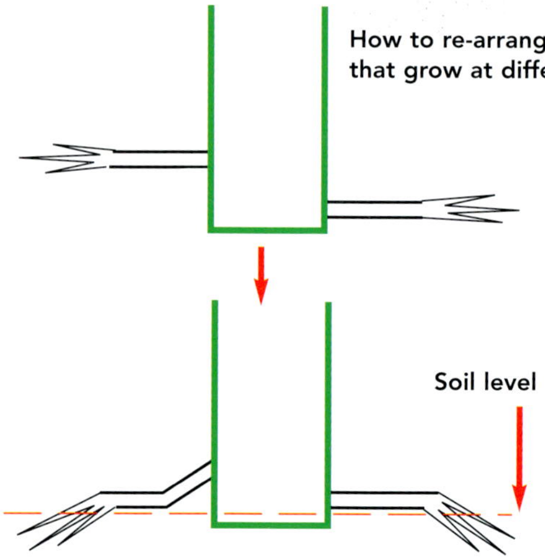

In this section we talk about horizontal roots, but in reality, these roots grow slightly downward. Because they grow as much out as down, there is no need to remove them. Their angle is the same as the slope of Mount Fuji, which is ideal in more ways than one!

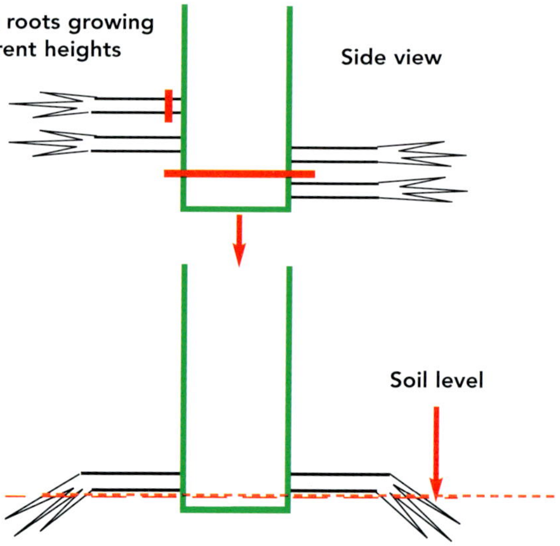

If the surface roots don't all come off the trunk at the same height, the problem can be solved by positioning them so that at least all their secondary roots enter the soil at the same level. This is fairly easy to accomplish when the roots are thin enough and they come off the trunk at close to the same height. In practice, you will always find trees whose roots, both thick and thin, grow at different heights and in different directions. If the roots grow at very different heights, more than 1" (2.5 cm) apart, a harmonious nebari will be hard to attain.

When there are several roots growing at different heights, it is best to arrange them so that the secondary roots are all at the same height. Sometimes not all the roots will cooperate; those that are too high or too low will have to go. If there are a lot of roots that need to be removed, remove them gradually over the course of several transplantings. If you remove them all at once, you may cause unnecessary stress.

An unglazed grey stoneware pot.

PREPARING THE POT

When the rootpruning is done, you are ready to pot. First, make sure your chosen pot is clean. Then fasten the drainage screen with short pieces of wire. Next secure the anchoring wire. The thickness of the anchoring wire depends upon the size of the tree. 3.0mm or 3.5mm is commonly used with most medium to large trees.

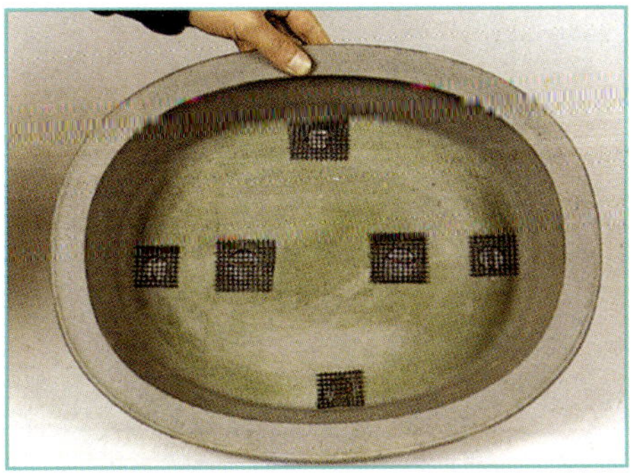

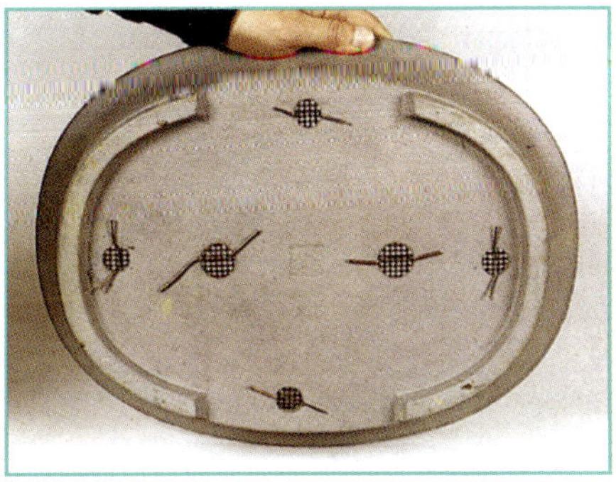

The screens are held in place with small pieces of wire.

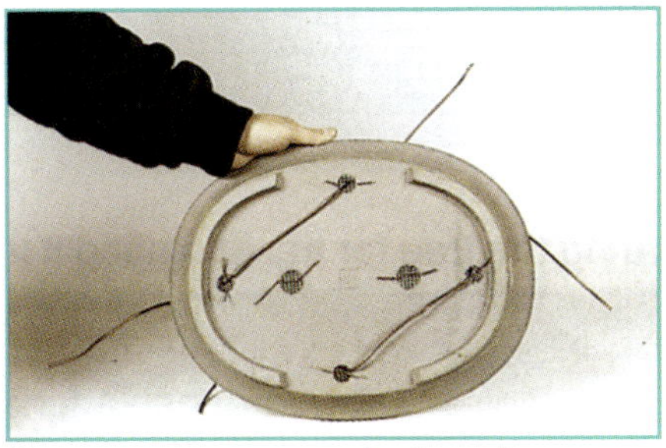

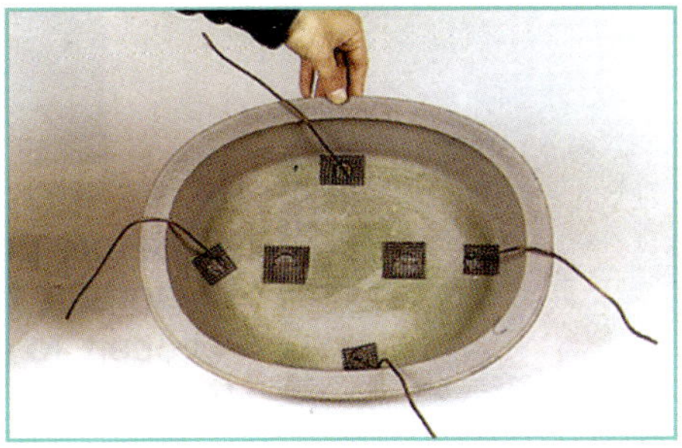

One way to secure anchoring wire.

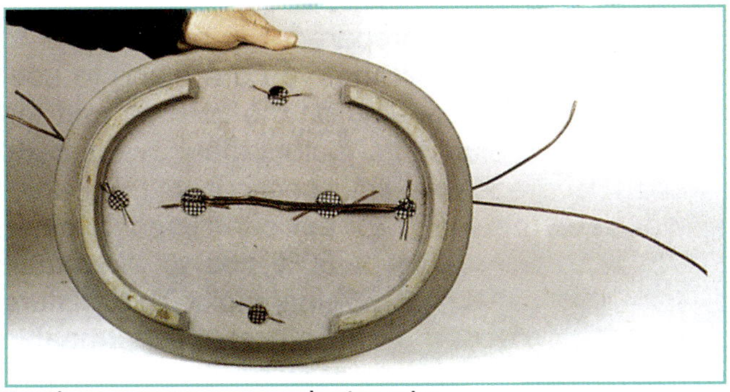

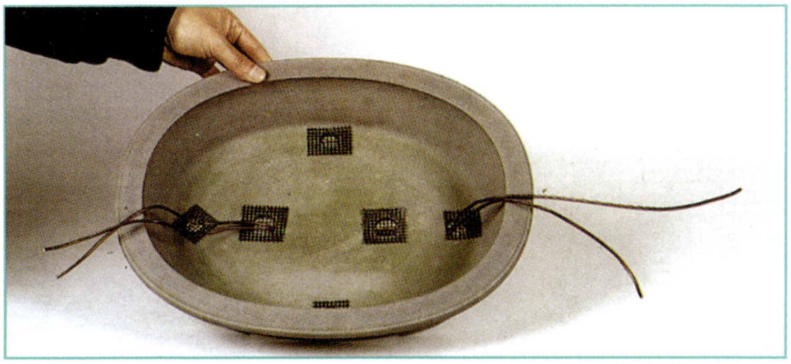

Another way to secure anchoring wire.

THE FINAL STEPS

Put your layer of drainage soil in the bottom of the pot. Almost all Japanese professionals use large soil particles in the bottom of the pot and smaller particles above those. Some growers even use three soils in layers, decreasing particle size as you go up. Some enthusiasts and growers in the west use only one size of particles and claim that the results are just as good. Ultimately, the choice is yours.

Make a conical mound of regular soil where you want the tree and place the tree on top of the mound. Gently twist the tree clockwise and counterclockwise to help the roots merge with the soil.

Next tie the rootball with the anchoring wire. Place rubber under the wire where it crosses any surface roots to avoid damage. Pull the wire tight until the tree is completely stable.

Now place the rest of the soil in the pot. Cover all the roots and later brush the soil off the nebari. Gently tap the side of the pot to help settle the soil. To eliminate air pockets, work a stick into the soil and gently rock it from side to side. Do this repeatedly, moving around the pot as you go.

Water thoroughly, until the water coming through the drainage holes runs clear. A good technique is to water for a few seconds, then wait a few seconds and water again. Do this several times to make sure all the soil is wet. Use a water soluble rooting compound to help the roots recover and grow.

First put the drainage layer in, and then make a conical mound of regular soil where you want to place the tree.

Make sure the anchoring wires are free.

Then place the tree and gently twist both ways to settle it onto the soil (this tree is a Japanese white pine).

Wire that comes directly into contact with roots can cause unnecessary damage. Use a piece of rubber to protect the roots.

Adding the rest of the soil.

Use a stick to eliminate air pockets.

Use a stick to push errant roots into the pot.

Brush the excess soil off.

Water thoroughly.

Our freshly potted tree. Though it still has a ways to go, it's off to a good start.

Another freshly repotted tree. If a bonsai could ever be finished, this magnificent old Japanese black pine would be. But a bonsai is never finished. Annual energy balancing is still necessary, and in a few years, it will need to be repotted again.

Pine from Seed

by Kusida Matsuo

Kusida Matsuo began growing bonsai in 1964. Like many western growers and enthusiasts, he started from scratch – first with collected seedlings and finally with collected seeds. In Japan most bonsai artists start with collected stock or nursery grown stock that is already quite developed. They leave the early stages to Mother Nature or to other growers. In this regard, Mr. Matsuo's methods are unique – and very useful. If you carefully follow the steps he presents, in a few short years you can have very impressive black pine bonsai (many of the techniques can be used for other varieties as well) that cost little more than the labor of love.

Kusida Matsuo, a pioneer black pine grower, has good reason to smile.

When I began growing bonsai professionally, everybody laughed at me. I wanted to start with the smallest investment possible and obtain high yield, quality bonsai material in a very short span of time. People thought I was joking, but I wasn't, and I succeeded.

Since I had no money, I decided I would have to grow my own trees from seed that I would collect myself. This required nothing more than a walk in the mountains with a sack and a keen eye for pine cones on parent trees that had the right characteristics.

Once I decided on collected seeds as the best way to start, I needed to figure out how to obtain rapid results with the seeds. After investigating and testing various ideas, I finally arrived at the method that is shown in these pages. This method effectively doubles the apparent age of trees, so that ten-year-old pines appear to be about twenty years old.

Not a good parent tree.

First, you need to carefully select the parent trees. Always choose mature trees so you can tell if they have desirable traits, like thick trunks and low compact branching. The best are those that are growing alone, rather than tall ones with all their branches in the crown that you find in thick forests. The best cones are those that grow on the dense south-facing branches.

It is important to look at a potential parent tree's shoots. If the bases of the shoots are bare, look somewhere else for pinecones. If the bases of the shoots have plenty of short, straight needles, you have come to the right place.

A good parent tree. The best parent trees are those that are growing alone, have abundant low compact branching, and dense needles that completely cover their shoots.

Always pick pinecones from the tree, not from the ground. Mid to late fall is the best time to do this. Collect only large cones with tight scales.

When you get the cones home, soak them for a day in a pail of water with some lime-sulphur added to clean up any fungi. Next dry the cones in the sun on screen or wire benches. When they are dry, open them and remove the seeds. Then separate the seeds from their little wings by rubbing some together between your hands.

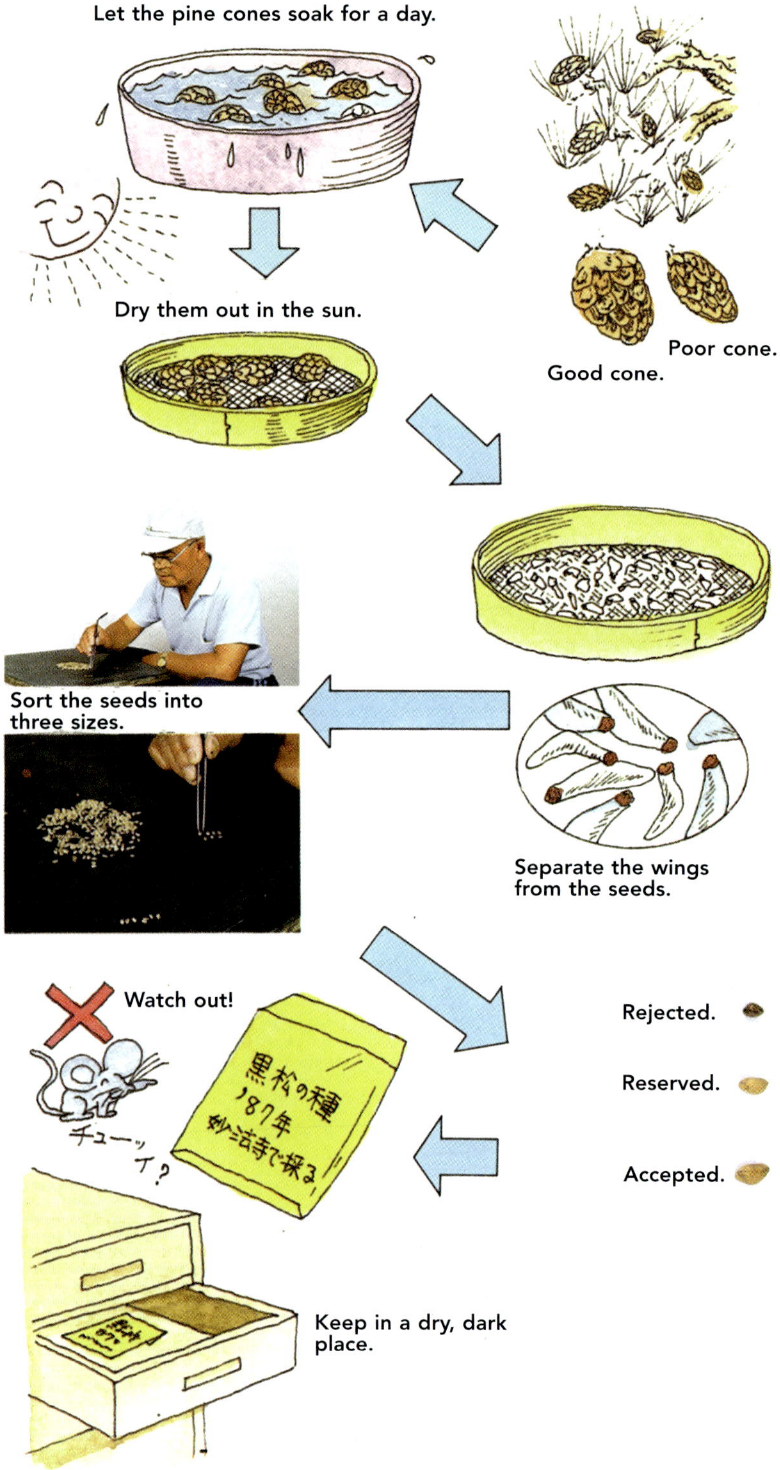

Next, select the largest healthiest looking seeds and put them in a brown paper bag (Mr. Matsuo separates the seeds into three groups: the largest, which he sows first, medium sized which he holds in reserve, and the smallest, which he throws away). Store the bag in a cool dry place that is protected from insects and critters.

Sow the seeds in early spring. First soak them for three days. Any that float are dead, so throw them away.

Use a plastic or wooden flat with good drainage. The soil you use should have excellent drainage. I use 80% river sand and 20% sterile sphagnum moss. Use a matchstick to make holes about 3/4" apart at a depth of about twice the thickness of a seed. Drop one seed in each hole, cover them with soil, and then move the flat to a sheltered spot out of direct sun and wind. Water thoroughly, then check the soil daily and water as soon as it becomes dry (no sooner, no later!). In ten or fifteen days you should see new plants peaking through the soil. A week or so later, most of them will begin to open out their needles.

Now alternate fungicide and vitamin B1 with each watering. As before, water only when the soil is dry. If the soil stays wet too long, you can tilt the tray by shimming one side. This should improve drainage.

Now comes the fun part. The little seedlings will have green stems when they first germinate. When the needles open, the stem color changes to a rosy color and then to a violet color. When the stems are violet, it is time to cut the roots.

Choose the seedlings that have the thickest straightest needles. With a gentle tug, pull the baby plants out of the soil. Take a razor blade and cut straight across the stems about 1″ below the needles. As soon as you cut one, place it into a pail of water and move on to the next one. *For a second optional cutting, see the accompanying diagram.*

Choose small plastic pots with excellent drainage to plant your seedlings. For the bottom layer of soil I use small stones, about 1/4″ to 3/8.″ I use the same mix I used before for the rest of the soil. If you like, you can use three grades of soil rather than two (see diagram).

Take the plants out of the water and powder each stem with a rooting compound (*if you prefer, you can use a liquid rooting compound when you water*). Plant one seedling in each pot. Leave 1/8″ to 1/4″ of each exposed above the soil line. Move the pots to a sheltered spot out of direct sun and wind and water thoroughly.

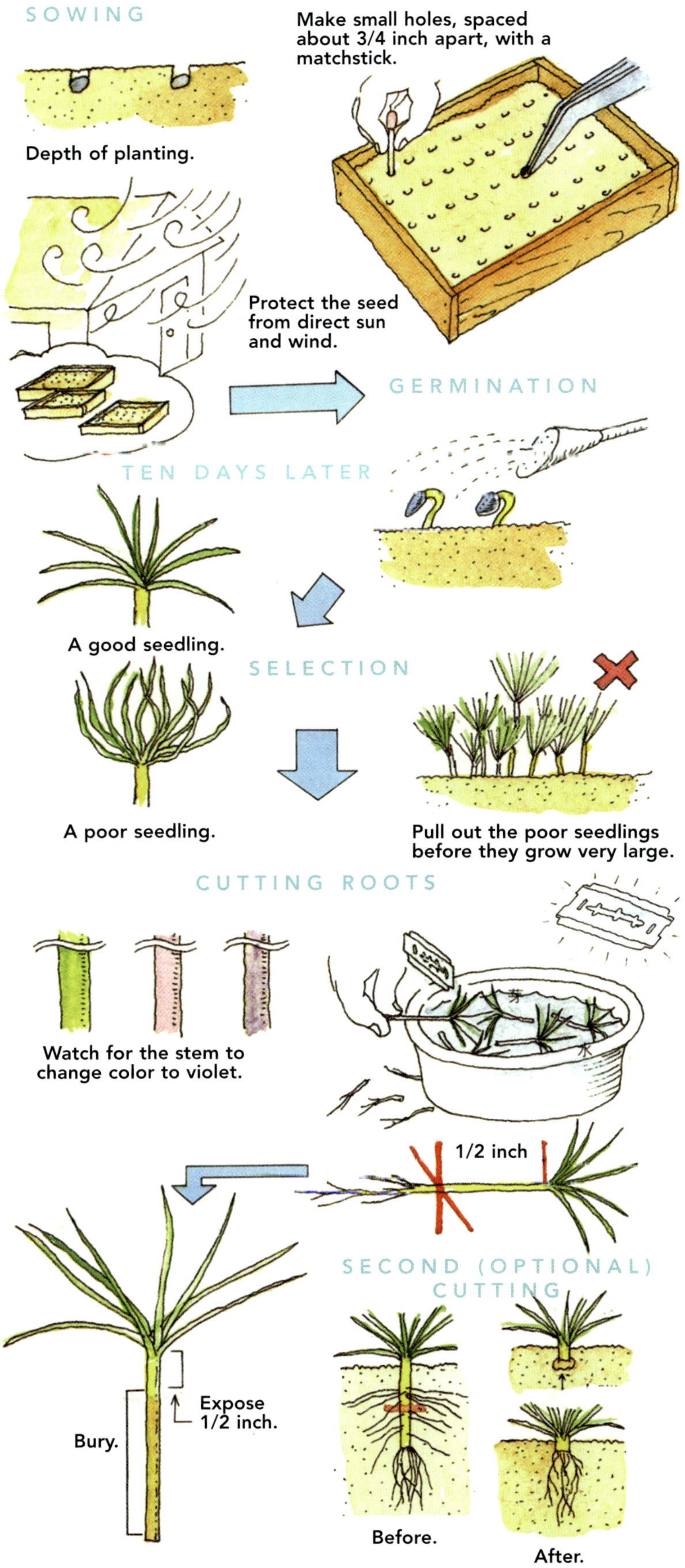

PLANTING THE CUTTINGS

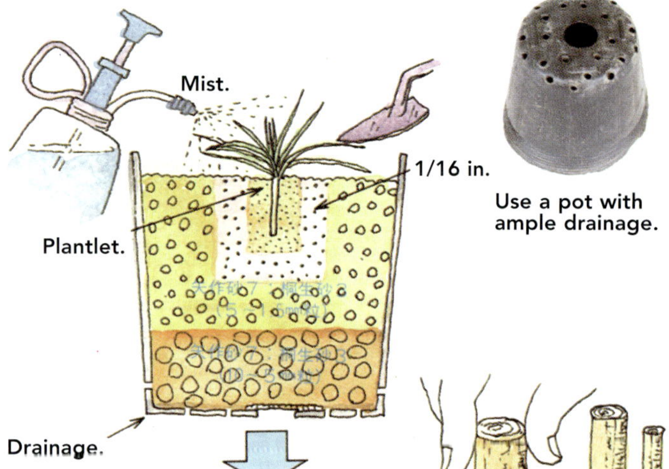

POST-TRANSPLANTING CARE

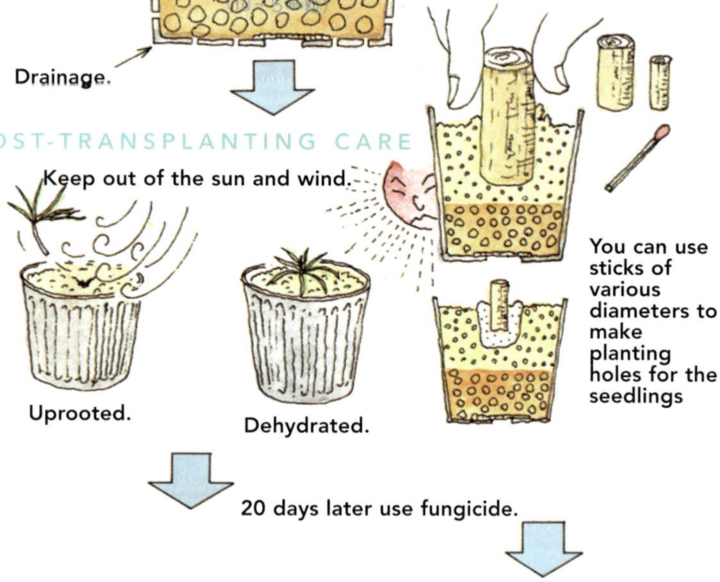

40 DAYS AFTER PLANTING

CARE IN WINTER

About six weeks after planting, you should begin to see little roots poking out the drain holes. When this happens, you don't want the pots sitting directly on the ground. I place mine on a bed of gravel so the roots don't sit in water.

Move the pots into the full sun and start fertilizing around July 10th. A well-balanced fertilizer with plenty of nitrogen is essential. I prefer organic slow release balls, specially formulated for bonsai. Three or four balls per pot will last the entire growing season (*Bio-gold triangles work well, though they are smaller, so you'll need to use more*). If you prefer liquid fertilizer, dilute to 1/2 strength and apply once a week until the fall.

Watering requirements will go up dramatically with vigorously growing plants in full sun. You may even need to water several times on hot days. If you've done everything right so far and continue to do things right, you'll have all the elements of the magic formula working together: sun + water + fertilizer + drainage = vigorous growth.

Around mid-fall, when the cold winds start, cover the plants with netting for winter protection. *If you live in a very cold climate, you'll need more than just netting.*

You can begin to shape with wire in the late winter or early spring. You'll probably need to remove a few lower needles to make room for the wire. Try not to disturb needles that have buds at their base. Use 3 or 3.5mm wire. Leave it on long enough for it to begin to score the bark (but not long enough for the bark to completely cover the wire). This will accelerate trunk thickening and the scars will heal soon enough. (*Mr. Matsuo recommends that you intentionally scar the trunk only with the first wiring – with subsequent wiring, be careful to avoid heavy scarring*). Continue to fertilize and water through the growing season.

You may have to remove some needles before you wire, but try not to damage any buds. In addition to shaping, wiring will help thicken the trunks, if the wire is left on long enough to scar the bark.

After the first wire has been removed. Scarring has accelerated thickening by about one year.

Don't coil the wire too tightly.

This way the branch can grow freely.

Normally you wouldn't remove so many needles. Here they have been removed so the shape of the trunk can be seen clearly.

The following year, in mid-spring, it is time to rootprune and transplant. Completely clean all the soil from the rootballs and cut off the thick roots, while leaving as many fine roots as you can. For pots, you are going to use something quite unusual — 6″ plastic colanders. The extra drainage and aeration works wonders for the formation of fine feeder roots, subsequent top growth and most importantly, trunk thickening. Another big plus with the colanders is that you don't have to worry about overwatering. The excess just runs right out.

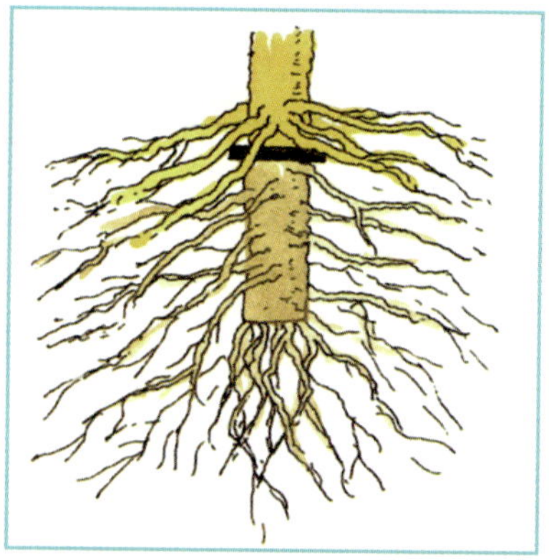

Prune away most of the lower roots. This promotes the horizontal growth and strong nebari that are so desirable for bonsai.

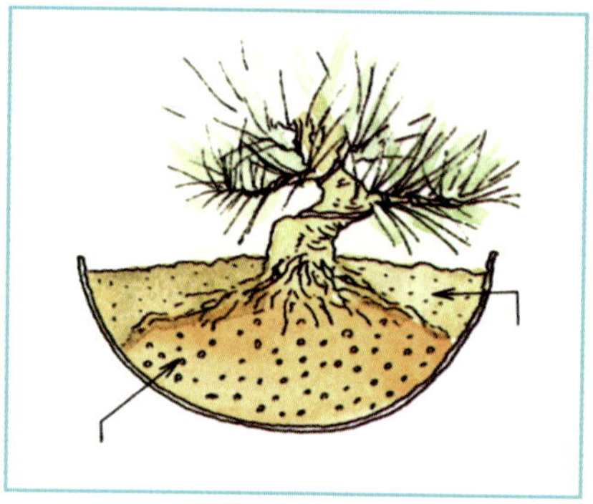

For soil, I use seven parts river sand and three parts akadama. Spread the roots evenly and plant in the middle of the colander. Apply a rooting compound. When the new roots grow through the holes they will stop elongating and push out more and more feeder roots along their lengths.

As before, water several times a day and use plenty of fertilizer. As the trees increase in size you can increase the amount of fertilizer you apply. If you use solid organic fertilizer, it may eventually form a hard crust on the soil. Check periodically and use a chopstick to break the crust up, so the soil can aerate. If you don't want to water several times a day, replace the akadama in your soil with kanuma. This will slow down the drainage. *It will also slow root growth down a little.*

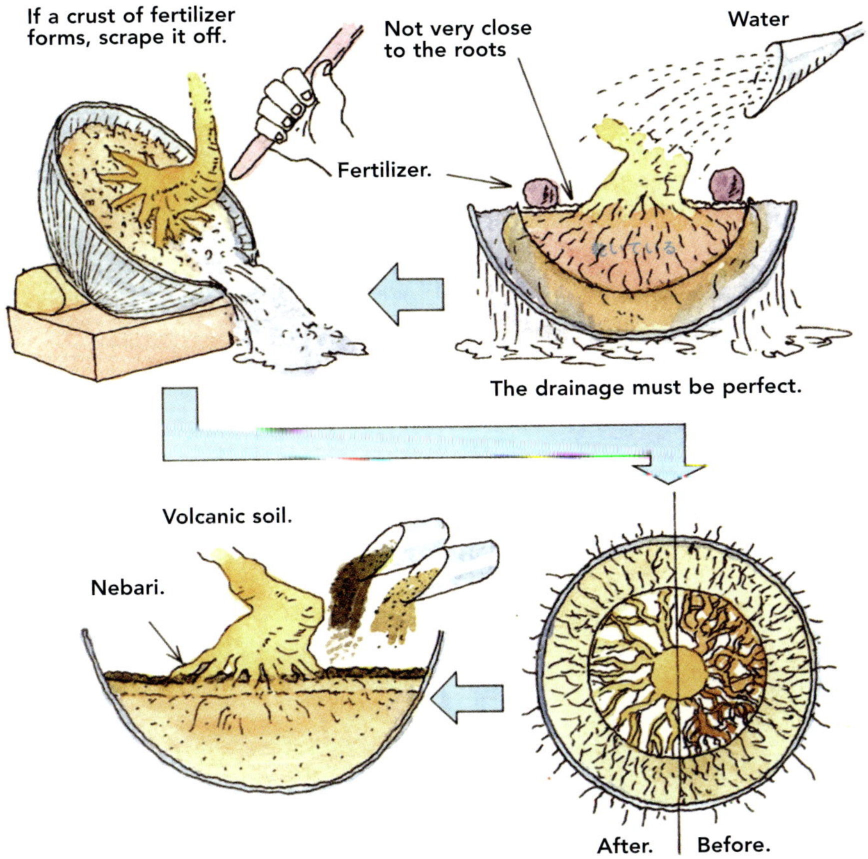

This scarring is too deep.
Due to intensive feeding, the trunks grow very rapidly. This can cause problems with wire cutting into the bark. With the first wiring, moderately scoring the bark is desirable — it encourages thickening. However, with subsequent wirings, you want to avoid too much scarring — the older a tree, the longer the scar marks last. Use plenty of fertilizer for thickening the trunks — but make sure to remove the wire in time.

Fertilizing. Year one: moderate dosage — four fertilizer balls. The small plastic cap is to keep the fertilizer in place and protect it from birds and other critters.

Year two: increased dosage, six balls.

Year five: ten to twelve balls.

Year nine: the soil is almost covered with fertilizer. Notice how none are too close to the trunk.

Don't forget to continue to wire to achieve the shapes you want. But be careful — now that your pines are growing more vigorously than ever, you'll need to check regularly to make sure the wire doesn't become embedded in the bark. You may need to unwire and rewire two or three times in one growing season.

The following year the trunks should be close to 2″ in diameter. It's time to move your trees into 8″ colanders. Put some drainage soil in first. Then place the 6″ colander, tree and all, into the 8″ colander and add some regular soil. This double colander technique will prevent any root disturbance so you don't lose any growing time. Staying with colanders has the added advantage of promoting excellent nebari growth.

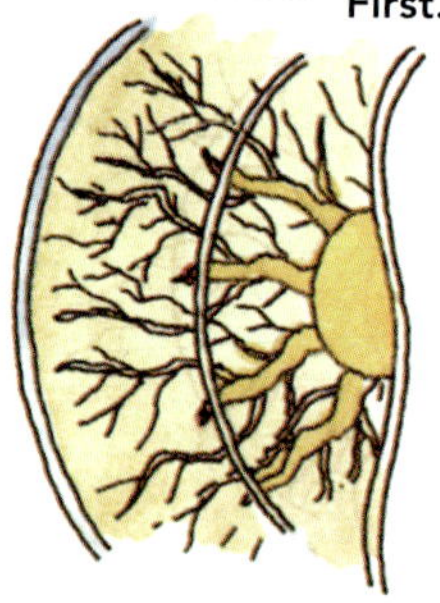

The double colander doesn't bother the roots.

Both colanders have the same soil mix.

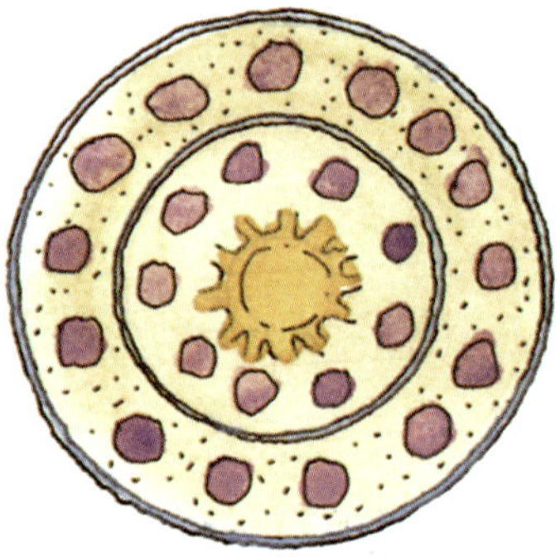

The fertilizer must be distributed evenly between the two colanders. If it is not, the roots in the central rootball will loose the strength they are going to need when the final transplanting is done.

Keep a deep drainage layer.

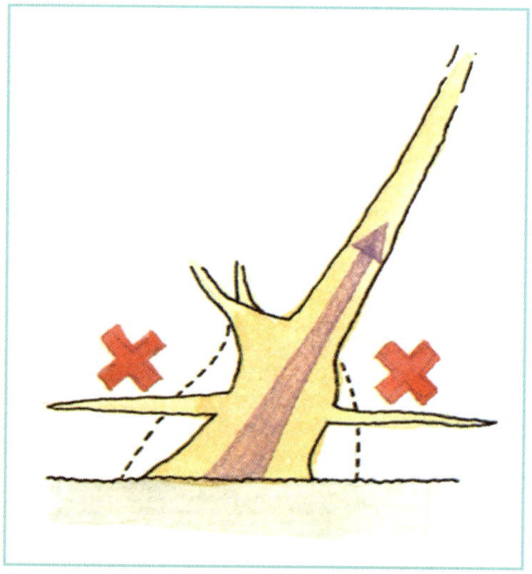

4th year. Time to move up to the larger colander. Now growth will be unstoppable. The Xs indicate the smaller branches whose growth will be slowed down because the leader is allowed to grow. This is fine for now, as you are primarily concerned with trunk development.

By now your trees are in their fourth year and they will have developed a long strong upper leader with some smaller branches down low. Though you might be tempted to cut the leader completely off to encourage the smaller branches, don't do it. If you let it continue to grow, it will accelerate the thickening of the trunk. Instead of cutting it off, shorten it to just above a branch. This branch will become the new leader. *This is the clip and grow styling method.* Now let this new leader grow freely.

Year two.

Year four.

In the fifth year you may be tempted to cut the apex off. Don't do it! Instead cut it down to its first lateral branch.

Fifth year.

Seventh year.

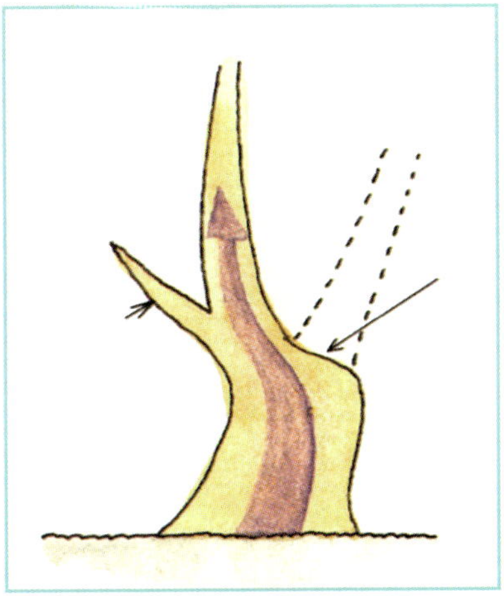
Change of leader.

View of new leader from above.

Appearance in the first year of training.

At the end of the fourth year, the trunk has thickened sufficiently to permit design pruning.

In June or July of year five, pinch back the lateral growth.

Some trunks may turn out straight.

Now you can wire the lateral branches.

The trunk is thickening nicely.

Now that it's in a bonsai pot, it's time to cut off the leader.

Mr. Matsuo decided to pot this sweet little shohin in a bonsai pot after only seven years. Many of his pines stay in training pots much longer. Height 4," diameter 1."

By the fifth year, some of your little trees will be getting ready for regular bonsai styling. In July, cut the leader back just as before, to just above a branch that will become the new leader. At the same time, pinch back the lowest branches to begin to create more density.

In April of the following year, remove the trees from their colanders. Remove all the soil and cut the roots back to where the walls of the smaller colander were. Then prune the remaining roots just as you would for any bonsai and place the trees in bonsai pots (or bonsai training pots) of your choice. Now protect your freshly potted bonsai from the sun and wind and wait for budding.

When fresh buds appear, cut the long leader off completely and wire the lateral branches. This is also the time to begin the annual process of balancing energy throughout the tree (see pages 109 & 111-117).

Here are some of Mr. Masuo's black pines that were grown from seeds. As you can see, the results are astounding, considering the time from seed. You'll notice that some are called *yatsubusa*. Loosely translated, *yatsubusa* means dwarf. At the time of the original article (1991), Mr. Matsuo was working on developing a consistent and sustainable supply of this dwarf variety. *Though the original Japanese article doesn't say, our guess is the yatsubusa variety is Mikawa (named after a region in Japan).*

Black pine. Seven years from seed. Height: 6 1/2", trunk diameter: 2 1/8"

Black pine. Six years from seed. Height: 4", trunk diameter: 1"

Black pine. Nine years from seed. Height: 10 1/2", trunk diameter: 2 3/4"

Yatsubusa black pine. Twelve years from seed. Height: 10 1/4", trunk diameter: 3 3/8"

Yatsubusa black pine. Eleven years from seed. Height: 11", trunk diameter: 3"

Yatsubusa black pine. Twenty years from seed. Height: 24", trunk diameter: 5 1/2"

Black pine. Eight years from seed. Height: 7 1/2", trunk diameter: 1 5/8"

Restyling

AN OLD BLACK PINE

Artist: Mitsuya Yasuo

The previous front. It is clear from its unkempt appearance that the needles, buds, candles and shoots have not been related to for several years.

Contrury to what some may believe, restyling a bonsai can be every bit as challenging as styling untouched material. In this chapter, Master Mitsuya Yasuo demonstrates how the original back can be transformed into a new, more appealing front.

Japanese terms in this section include: Moyogi - informal upright style, Chokkan - formal upright style, Nebari - Surface roots.

JOURNEY THROUGH GENERATIONS

Bonsai do not belong to us; it is our responsibility to care for them and pass them on to future generations. The Japanese black pine is one of our favorites. Because it can live and remain healthy for several hundred years, it is an excellent subject for the journey through the generations.

The black pine is one of the hardiest species used for bonsai, provided you live in a zone without intense freezes and use a soil mix that drains well. Because it grows vigorously, the black pine requires persistent and methodical care to keep its needles at a reasonable scale for bonsai. The tree in this chapter was allowed to grow uncontrolled for three years. The needles grew too long and the low areas began to lose strength. However, with a little effort, we can return it to scale and perhaps even improve it in the process.

This pine has been a bonsai for 40 years, so it is impossible to bend the trunk and very difficult to bend any of the three primary branches. Restyling can best be accomplished by studying and changing the front, changing its position in the container, pruning select buds and shoots, and extensive wiring of the medium and small diameter branches.

Since it is a black pine, we can restyle and transplant it immediately. If this were a five-needle pine (*white pine*), the whole process would take at least two years. Even so, restyling this tree will not be easy. When a tree is trained as a bonsai for many years, its growth rings grow very close together. With each passing year the trunk and branches become more rigid. This makes them more and more difficult to bend without breaking.

continued page 157

Restyling bonsai that have been neglected for years can be difficult, especially if you are working with Japanese black pine. Here's a technique for working with rigid older branches you might find useful.

1. Wrap the inflexible branch or trunk with wet raffia.

2. Attach a length of annealed copper wire as a spine on the outside of the proposed bend with a few strands of raffia (you can use aluminum wire if you don't have solid copper, but it's not as strong).

3. Rewrap the spine and raffia with black electrical tape.

4. Coil annealed copper wire along the entire branch, using regular wiring technique (again, you can use aluminum wire).

5. Slowly and carefully bend the branch into the desired position. If necessary, apply a guy wire to secure the branch in its new position.

This technique will work on branches up to 2 inches in diameter if you are patient and careful. Larger diameter branches usually require a lever to bend. We've seen very heavy trunks moved in stages using levers. Patience and care are the keys.

SELECTING A FRONT

The trunk

The trunk is the most important feature on most bonsai. Everything else plays off the trunk. The first things to look for are taper and line. The ideal trunk is one that tapers from the base to the top, and has interesting curves or lines (the exception, when it comes to line, is chokkan – formal upright style – where the trunk is always straight). Though the nebari and the branching (and other features) will influence your decision, always consider both taper and line when choosing a front.

Often trunks will have defects other than bad taper or poor lines. Heavy scarring is the most common. The first question to ask yourself about a defect is: will it heal and diminish over time? If the answer is no, then the next question is, can it be transformed into something beautiful, like a shari (a section of natural-looking dead wood)? If the answer is still no, then the next question is, can you hide it? If the answer is still no, then you might want to consider a different tree.

The nebari

Some people start with the nebari when selecting a pine, as a good nebari is hard to come by and can profoundly effect the overall appearance of a tree. We've always thought that the trunk is the first thing to look at, but there is no question that, with pines, the nebari is very important.

Frequently, the nebari will be covered by soil or moss, so you need to start by gently raking the surface area surrounding the trunk. When you have exposed the nebari, rotate the tree so you can see the root configuration from different perspectives. Also, try tilting the tree at various angles to find the best exposure.

Although the ideal nebari will radiate out from the trunk in all directions, this is not commonly found in raw material. Sometimes the existing position of the surface roots can be altered by separating and relocating the roots, then holding them in place with u-shaped wire pins. For more on developing a nebari, see pages 132 - 136.

To properly evaluate your tree's surface roots, visualize your planned design. For example, if you are considering a shakan (slanting) style with the tree leaning to the left, strong roots on the right side of the trunk will be helpful. The nebari should emphasize the tree's connection to the earth. In this chapter, the right-sided nebari supports the position of the tree.

If you are considering a chokkan (formal upright) style, roots on all sides of the trunk reinforce the sense of uniformity and stability of the style. This is also true of the moyogi (informal upright) style, though here you have more flexibility with the shape of the nebari.

Branch Placement

The next step in determining the front of the bonsai is evaluating how the branches are arranged. The rule of thumb is that the first (or lowest, and usually longest and thickest) branch should be at approximately 1/3 the height of the tree and should be either on your left or your right as you face the front. The remaining branches should ideally step up the trunk by alternating from side to side and back, with some branches in the front starting about 2/3 of the way up the trunk. The branches should diminish in length and thickness from bottom to top. Though a perfect arrangement is not the goal, this basic configuration provides a good starting point.

Other considerations include the presence of extra filler or back branches, which add depth to your design by creating a rhythm of solids and voids (branches and space).

The top

The top of the tree is commonly overlooked when choosing a front. The basic rule is that the crown should tilt towards the viewer. Often we will ignore the top because it is the easiest to correct. Wiring, trimming and time can almost always correct a crown that leans the wrong way. Still, it's a plus if you can find a top that is already leaning forward.

Summary

Selecting a front is almost always a compromise, as you seldom find a tree that has all, or even most of its best features facing the same way. From one angle the trunk might be defective, and from a slightly different angle it might be quite strong and flawless, although from the first angle the branching or nebari are better. And so it goes. All you can do is weigh all the factors, make your decision, and start to work, with the understanding that your view may change as you become more familiar with the tree.

The new front. The line of the trunk is much more visible and the primary branch is more graceful from this view.

CHOOSING THE FRONT

This black pine will work with either its present front or back as the front. Its previous owner planted it in the center of the pot, almost as if he could not decide. We prefer the side with the hanging branch falling to the left. This view shows off more of the trunk. *Though you generally want to expose the bottom third of the trunk, this trunk is so flawless and has bark that is so well-aged and beautiful, that Mr. Kasan chooses to expose much more than just the bottom third.*

The previous owner chose the opposite front, evident from the fact that the crown inclines in that direction. Because we're selecting the other side, we must change the entire crown so that it leans toward the new front.

REWORKING THE BRANCHES

Our new front requires us to take another look at the primary branch. A hanging branch is usually very attractive, but on this tree it goes largely unnoticed, hidden behind its own foliage. It is too old and rigid to wire and change its shape, so the only solution is to remove or jin (*jin is the final solution*) the small secondary branch that grows inward toward the trunk and to thin out the remaining foliage.

We repeat the process with the rest of the branches on the left side, leaving the strong shoots and removing the weak ones, then pruning and wiring so that all the shoots will receive ample light. The right side is more challenging – the trunk grows to the left with all the branches on that side hanging downward. Reducing the foliage on the right will create an imbalance. Leaving the right side too dense will rob needed strength from the left. *Cascading branches tend to receive less energy than branches closer to the apex. For more on this see cascade chapter page 118.*

The solution is to lower the first branch on the right. *Lowering it will create a visual counter-balancing weight to the cascading branch on the other side.* To get such an tough old branch to move, we have to partially break it. This process is shown in detail in the accompanying photos.

We tie on some raffia where we expect the branch to break. Binding the area firmly supports the branch so it won't move after it's cracked, which is essential for healing. Next we lower the branch using a metal bar that is bound to the base of the branch with wire. The bar is braced against the bottom of an upper curve in the trunk so it can be used as a lever. When the branch is where we want it, we secure it with a guy wire that we attach to the primary branch on the opposite side on the tree.

Using rebar is becoming quite common with bonsai artists and enthusiasts. If you decide to try it, be careful. It's easy to completely break a branch if you use too much force. Make sure you protect the branch with raffia. You can also use a wire spine and electrical tape in conjunction with using a rebar lever.

Mr. Mitsuya uses jin pliers on a secondary branch.

Side view.

Opposite side. Note how the apex is inclined toward the previous front.

Note how foliage on the primary branch partially hides the trunk.

Now the unwanted foliage has been removed and part of the primary branch is ready to jin.

Voila! A beautiful jin.

The primary branch has been wired and pulled closer to the trunk with a small guy wire.

After pruning and removing some needles, meticulous wiring on every branch, even the smallest, is necessary.

The tree is too unstable. It needs a counterbalancing weight on the right.

The arrow shows where the first right branch needs to come down to balance the weight on the left side of the tree.

A close-up. The section of branch that is most likely to break is wrapped with raffia.

Then a piece of rebar is fastened to the branch and braced against the trunk.

The bar is used as a lever and the branch is lowered.

The branch to be bent after the raffia has been applied.

Rebar is used as a lever.

After bending the branch is tied down with guy wire.

Next the secondary branches are pruned and wired.

Branches are opened up into desirable fan shapes. This allows more light into the center of the tree.

By simply by lowering the first right branch, the tree seems much better balanced.

A REDESIGNED APEX

Our next step is correcting the apex so it nods toward the new front. When we open up the crown, we discover that the actual apex consists of only three branches. We also discover that the trunk is thicker near the apex than we would like. Though there is little we can do about its thickness, we can reshape it using heavy copper wire. The apex is the most vigorous area of the tree, so we remove all the strong shoots and leave only two or three pairs of needles on the remaining shoots.

The author inspects the apex.

The photos above show two sequences (each from left to right) of the results of the stages of pruning and wiring, and shoot and needle removal.

The is the front the author was considering.

This is the front he finally chooses. Changing one's mind as a project evolves is quite common.

TIME FOR A NEW POT

Once the top is completed, it's time to transplant into a new round pot. The previous pot measured 22 x 15 x 3 inches (56 x 39 x 8 cm); the new pot measures 15 inches (38 cm) in diameter by 3 inches (8 cm) in depth. Transplanting is the time to adjust the planting angle. In order to bring the apex a little more toward the front, we raise the trunk into a slightly more vertical position. *This not only brings the apex forward, it also creates more visual stability.*

A peek back at what we started with.

Literati pot, literati tree?

After restyling and repotting, this tree might now be considered a literati (bunjin) style tree, or at least a tree that tends towards literati style. The round drum pot (see next page) further emphasizes the literati aspects (drum pots are often used for literati trees). For more on literati style, see page 79.

SUMMARY

1. Study your tree thoroughly before deciding on the front. Evaluate the nebari, trunk line, branch locations, the apex and the overall inclination of the tree.

2. Don't be afraid to reverse what someone else has done. Like all living things, bonsai change over time. What was once the optimal front may later become the back.

3. Balancing energy is essential, especially with pines. Though your pine may look a little peculiar right after you have thinned out excess growth, pinched the candles and pulled needles, this is necessary if you want a quality pine bonsai. For a more complete discussion of energy balancing in black pines, see pages 110 to 117.

4. You can use a rebar lever to move stubborn old branches, provided you carefully follow all the necessary steps.

After repotting. With a little more refining and filling out, this tree will be ready to show.
Height, 28″ (71 cm). Round drum pot with nails.

Black Pine Gallery

Fudo, a famous and very old black pine that was collected on the island of *Setonai-kai* in 1961. Its current owner is Toshinori Suzuki.
Height 31″ (79 cm).
Trunk diameter 10″ (25 cm).

Another famous black pine with a long and storied history (see *Bonsai Today* 32). Its double hanging branches are quite unique and distinctive, and make it immediately recognizable. In 1993, when this photo was taken, its owner was Masahiro Tokuo. The artist at the time was Master Nakayatsu, a disciple of Saburo Kato. Height 32" (81 cm).

It's hard to tell where the rock ends and the trunk begins on this award winning root-over-rock black pine. Artist Toru Suzuki. Height 25" (63 cm).

This old black pine's massive trunk, nebari and cascading branch, as well as its distinctive shari and full crown make for a very powerful bonsai. Combined with the outrageously gnarled root-stand, it creates a very formidable display. This photo originally appeared on the cover of *Bonsai Today* 64. Estimated height 14" (36 cm).

Richly textured bark and a massive 9" (23 cm) diameter trunk are two of features that distinguish this old tree. The grey pot blends perfectly with the highlights on the bark. Height 32" (82 cm).

At first glance, this semi-cascade shohin black pine looks like a full-sized bonsai, but it's actually only 9" (23 cm) tall. The trunk almost spans the width of the tiny pot, and it's hard to imagine that so little soil could support such a powerful tree. Height 9" (23 cm).

A corked-bark Japanese black pine (*Pinus thunbergii* Corticosa) with a distinctively twisted trunk, immediately after it was restyled and transplanted by Akio Kondo. A stick props up one branch on the crown, while a guy-wire pulls another down. Height 28" (71 cm). Tokoname drum pot, 17" by 3.5" (43 by 9 cm).

The wire and fresh jins immediately tell us that this powerfully rugged little black pine was just restyled. The artist is Michiyo Akagi, one of the few well-known female bonsai artists in Japan. Height 11" (28 cm).

All we know about this old black pine (from Bonsai Today issue 90) is that it was an award winner at a Japanese National Style Exhibition. It's easy to see why — with its powerful nebari and trunk, striking bark and harmonious overall shape, it would be hard to pass by.

This famous black pine is one of the most striking examples of cascading bonsai anywhere. The powerful slanting trunk and apex alone would make an exceptional tree — when you add the remarkably long and beautiful cascade, you have something truly unique. In addition to all this, the expertise in balancing and care that is required just to keep such a low cascading branch healthy is quite impressive. Originally appeared on the cover of Bonsai Today 76. Height unknown.

Glossary of Bonsai Terms

ACCENT PLANT Also called a companion plant. A small plant placed next to a bonsai.

ADVENTITIOUS BUDS Buds that appear at unexpected or unusual locations. These can be useful when attempting to force back-budding.

AIR LAYERING A propagation technique to develop roots on a branch. When the roots are developed, the branch is cut off and planted.

AKADAMA A red clay soil from Japan. Commonly used for pines and other conifers.

APEX The highest point on a bonsai.

BACK-BUDDING Developing buds on old wood. Back-budding can sometimes be forced by drastic pruning.

BUD With pines, we only speak of one type of bud; those that are future shoots. The sequence is bud, candle, shoot and branch.

BUNJIN OR BUNJIN-GI Also called literati style. A bonsai characterized by a long, usually thin trunk, with lots of movement, and most, or all, of the branching and foliage on the top third of the tree.

CAMBIUM Green layer of tissue (one cell thick) between the bark and the sapwood of trees.

CANDLE An elongated bud. On pines, buds elongate into candles in the spring. Later in the spring and summer, candles open and elongate into shoots.

CANDLE PINCHING Refers to either completely removing or shortening candles in order to develop shorter needles and balance energy.

CASCADE STYLE *Kengai* in Japanese. A bonsai that grows downward, with its tip below the base of the pot.

CORK-BARKED JAPANESE BLACK PINE *Nishiki matsu* in Japanese. Black pine cultivars (there are several different *nishiki matsu* cultivars) that have corky bark. Good ones are rare in the west. Also sometimes called 'winged pines'.

CROWN The top part of a bonsai. Sometimes used interchangeably with apex, though more accurately used to refer to the whole upper foliage mass and supporting upper branches.

CULTIVAR A subspecies that has been developed by humans. An example is: *Pinus parviflora 'Zuisho'* (Japanese white pine, *Zuisho*). Cultivars are often referred to as varieties, though varieties is a broader term that includes naturally occurring plants and plants developed by humans.

DIEBACK The death of shoots or branch tips, caused by disease or pests. If the cause isn't dealt with, the entire plant can die.

DORMANCY When a tree is resting and growth is inactive. Winter dormancy is common in cold climates. In very hot climates, trees can experience summer dormancy.

FIELD GROWN STOCK Plants that are grown in the ground, usually for commercial purposes. Distinguished from container grown nursery stock and plants collected from the wild.

FORMAL UPRIGHT STYLE *Chokkan* in Japanese. A bonsai style characterized by a straight vertical trunk with an even taper and evenly alternating branches.

GOYOMATSU Japanese white pine, *Pinus parviflora*.

HABIT Typical growth pattern of a tree. Examples: spreading, conical.

INFORMAL UPRIGHT STYLE *Moyogi* in Japanese. Like the formal upright, the apex is on the same vertical axis as the trunk (more or less in this case). Unlike the formal upright, the trunk is not straight, nor is the branching necessarily symmetrical.

INTERNODE The distance between two nodes. Nodes are where buds appear. In bonsai, short internodes are desirable.

JIN A dead branch that is stripped of its bark and developed for design purposes. Jins can occur naturally or can be manmade. Jins are usually treated with lime-sulphur to prevent rotting.

KUROMATSU Japanese black pine, *Pinus thunbergii*.

LITERATI STYLE Also called *bunjin*. A bonsai characterized by a long, usually thin trunk, with lots of movement, and most, or all, of its branching and foliage on the top third of the tree.

MACRO-NUTRIENTS Nutrients that are necessary (in fairly large quantities) for a plant's survival and health. Nitrogen, phosphorous and potassium (NPK) are commonly known macro-nutrients. Some sources also list carbon, oxygen, hydrogen, calcium, sulphur and magnesium as macro-nutrients.

MICRO-NUTRIENTS Elements that are required in very small amounts for a plant's health; for example, iron.

MAME A bonsai less than 3" (7 cm) tall.

MASAKUNI The original bonsai tool manufacturer, and producer of the largest assortment of bonsai tools in the world. Masakuni tools are generally renowned for high quality by enthusiasts and professionals .

MULTIPLE-TRUNK OR CLUMP STYLE A group of trunks growing from a single root system. The Japanese term is *kabudachi.*

MYCORRHIZA An symbiosis of plants and mycorrhizal fungi. The fungi adhere to roots and help the plant absorb water and essential nutrients. Pines are particularly dependent on mycorrhizal fungi.

MUCK A mix of clay (or akadama dust) and peat, sphagnum moss or sometimes other ingredients, that is used to make walls for holding soil on rock plantings.

NEAGARI Exposed root style bonsai; where roots form the trunk. Roots are usually exposed by periodically removing some surface soil. Not to be confused with nebari.

NEBARI Surface roots that radiate out from the base of the trunk. On pines and many other bonsai varieties, a well developed nebari is highly desirable.

NEEDLE A narrow, cylindrical leaf.

NEEDLE CLUSTER Groups of two to five needles growing out of one sheath. All black pines have two needles per cluster and all white pines have five. Needle clusters are also called bundles.

NEEDLE PLUCKING Removing old needles, usually by the cluster, but sometimes by the needle. Used to help air and light get to the center of a tree, and to help balance a tree's energy.

NPK A code used to show the percentage of nitrogen, phosphorus and potassium in a fertilizer. For example, an NPK of 10-5-10, would indicate 10% nitrogen, 5% phosphorus and 10% potassium. These three elements are called macro-nutrients and are essential to the health of any plant.

OLD WOOD Woody growth that is more than a year old.

PENJING Chinese landscape planting. Sometimes translated as 'Chinese bonsai.'

PINUS PARVIFLORA Japanese white pine. *Goyomatsu* in Japanese.

PINUS THUNBERGII Japanese black pine. *Kuromatsu* in Japanese.

PRIMARY BRANCH Also called the main branch. The longest and thickest branch. Usually the lowest branch (first branch).

PRIMARY BRANCHES Branches that grow off the trunk. Secondary branches grow off primary branches. The Primary branch (entry above) is one of the primary branches.

PROPAGATION How plants are started. Some ways that plants are propagated for bonsai are: from seed, by cutting, by grafting, by air-layering, by separation (e.g. trunks from a single root system), by tissue culture.

RAFT STYLE A type of forest bonsai that is created by laying a trunk down, partly or completely beneath the soil. Its old roots support it while it grows new roots along its length. What were previously branches become the trunks of the forest. The Japanese name is *ikadabuki*.

RAMIFICATION Ramifying literally means dividing, spreading or branching. A well-ramified tree would be a tree with good branching. A well-ramified branch would be a branch with good secondary branching. Ramification is also sometimes used when discussing roots.

ROOTBALL The roots and the soil that adheres to the roots, when a plant is removed from a pot or from the ground.

ROOTBOUND Also called potbound. When the roots have taken up all (or almost all) of the air space in a pot. Bonsai should be transplanted before they become completely rootbound.

ROOTSTOCK Roots (and usually the lower trunk) that are used for grafting. The part that is grafted onto rootstock is called the scion. White pine scions are frequently grafted onto black pine rootstock (usually with several inches of black pine trunk).

SACRIFICE BRANCH A branch that is used to help thicken part or all of a trunk or other branches. Sacrifice branches can also be used to strengthen a weak or under-developed section of a tree. They work by drawing energy into an area and are usually allowed to grow unimpeded. When the desired result has been achieved, the sacrifice branch is removed (sacrificed).

SAIKEI Landscape planting.

SECONDARY BRANCHES Branches that grow off of primary branches. Tertiary branches grow off of secondary branches.

SEMI- CASCADE STYLE A bonsai that grows horizontally and somewhat downward. With full cascades, the tip of the cascade grows below the base of the pot, while semi-cascade tips are above the base of the pot. Semi-cascade is sometimes called windswept style. This is not always accurate, as not all semi-cascades are windswept, and not all windswept trees are semi-cascade. The Japanese term is *han kengai.*

SHARI Deadwood on a trunk, that is developed for design purposes. Shari can occur naturally or can be manmade by carving. Shari is usually treated with lime-sulfur to prevent rot.

SHOHIN Bonsai up to 8" (20 cm) tall.

SHOOTS New growth that will become branches. The sequence with pines is buds, candles, shoots and branches.

SINUOUS ROOT STYLE Where a group of trunks grow from one long sinuous horizontal root. The Japanese term is *netsuranari*. Sinuous root style forests are often Japanese white pines.

SLANT STYLE A bonsai style where the trunk slants at approximately 45 degrees. *Shakan* in Japanese.

SLOW-RELEASE FERTILIZERS Solid fertilizers that are placed on the soil surface and release their nutrients over a period of time. Slow-release fertilizers are often organic and are commonly used on bonsai in the form of cakes, pellets, balls or triangles.

SPHAGNUM MOSS A type of moss found and harvested in bogs. Used as a component of muck and for air-layering.

SUIBAN A shallow dish without drainage holes. Often used for suiseki or ikebana.

SUISEKI Viewing stones. Chinese viewing stones are called *Gong-shi.*

SUPERFEEDING An aggressive fertilizing program developed by Michael Persiano.

SYSTEMIC A type of insecticide or fungicide that enters a plant's system through the roots and is carried throughout the plant via the sap.

TAPER Gradual narrowing as you move away from the base. In bonsai, good taper on trunks and branches is an important design feature. An example of good taper would be a trunk that is wide at the base and then gradually narrows as it ascends.

TAPROOT A single long, strong root that acts as an anchor by growing straight down.

TERTIARY BRANCHES Branches that grow off of secondary branches.

TOKONAME POTS Tokoname is a region in Japan that produces some of the best and most famous bonsai pots in the world. Many of the pines shown in this book and in ***Bonsai Today*** magazine, are in Tokoname pots.

TOKONOMA Traditional Japanese display area. Tokonomas will often have a bonsai with a scroll and a companion plant. Other elements can also be used.

VARIETY A general term often used to refer to a species or a subspecies. Frequently used interchangeably with cultivar, though varieties is a broader term that covers plants that occur naturally, as well as cultivars.

WINDSWEPT STYLE BONSAI A bonsai styled to give the appearance of a tree exposed to incessant winds. *Fukinagashi* in Japanese.

WINTER KILL The death of a plant or part of a plant caused by extreme cold and cold winds.

YATSUBUSA A variety exhibiting dwarfed characteristics, e.g., '*Mikawa*' Japanese Black Pine.

ZUISHO A short-needled Japanese white pine cultivar.

Japanese Bonsai Terms

AKADAMA TSUCHI Akadama soil.

AKAMATSU Red pine.

AMAI To water generously.

ARAKAWA SHO Tree with rough bark.

ARAKI OR ARAGI Freshly dug tree or new tree.

ATAMA Crown or apex of a tree.

BANKAN Trunk with many curves.

BANKON Fused root base.

BONKEI Tray landscape containing rocks and small accent plants as well as trees.

BUNJIN GI A bonsai with a long, thin trunk, with lots of movement, and top-heavy foliage.

CHOKKAN Formal upright style.

CHU Bonsai between 40 and 60 cm in height.

DAI Bonsai over 60 cm in height.

DAI KI Parent tree; stock.

DOU BUKI Adventitious budding.

EDA BONE Branch structure.

EDA BURI Branch arrangement.

EDA TANYA Branch shelf.

EDA NUKE Branch elimination.

FUKINAGASHI Windswept style.

GI SEI SHI Sacrifice branch.

GORO TSUCHI Coarse soil.

GOYOMATSU Japanese white pine.

HA GARI Pinching out leaves.

HA MIZU Misting.

HAN KENGAI Semi-cascade.

HARI GANE KAKE Wiring a tree.

HOKIDACHI Broom style.

ICHI NO EDA Number one branch.

IKADABUKI Raft style.

IKI MICHI Lifeline or water intake.

IMI EDA Non-essential branches.

ISHI SEKI Planted on rock.

ISHITSUKI Clinging to a rock or rock grown.

JIDAI Period or age.

JIN Deadwood branch.

JU SEI Growth of the tree or tree's vigor.

KANUMA TSUCHI Kanuma soil, commonly used for azaleas.

KABUDACHI Multiple trunk/clump style.

KANNUKI EDA An ugly branch that must be cut off.

KANSUI Watering.

KANJU Deciduous tree.

KARAI To water sparingly

KARAMI NE Tangled roots or intertwining of roots.

KARI KOMI Pruning of leaves and branches.

KARUSU Callous.

KATA EDA One-sided branching, as found in fukinagashi style (windswept).

KATA NE One-sided rooting.

KENGAI Cascade.

KENSEKI Rare stone.

KIFU Bonsai between 20 and 40 cm in height.

KIRI KOMI Trim; prune trunk, branches, or leaves to shape tree.

KIRI MODOSHI Cut back to first or second bud to promote ramification.

KOKEJUN Taper.

KUROMATSU Japanese black pine.

KYOKU DUKE Curve in the trunk or branches made by wiring.

MAME Bonsai less than 7 cm in height.

MI MONO Fruit bearing tree.

MI SHO MONO Bonsai from seed.

MI SHO Raising bonsai from seed.

MIZU GIRE Too dry (soil requires water).

MOYOGI Informal upright style.

MOYO Shape of the trunk.

NE BUSE Rootpruning.

NEBARI Trunk base and surface roots.

NEAGARI Exposed root style.

NETSUNAGARI Root connected.

NETSURANARI Sinuous root style.

NI NO EDA The second branch.

NIRE Elm.

NISHIKI MATSU Cork barked pine.

OKI HI Manure in pellet form.

OYAKO SOU KAN Two trunks growing from one root (mother and child).

PENWAN, PENZAI, Penjing Landscape planting. From the Chinese Penjing.

ROU BOKU Old, antique bonsai.

SABAMIKI Split trunk.

SAIKEI Landscape planting.

SAKU Composition; result of work done on a tree.

SANKAN Triple trunk.

SASHI HO A cutting.

SASHI EDA The longest and thickest branch that accentuates the tree.

SASHIKI Grown from cuttings.

SEISHI Bonsai training.

SEKI KAZARI Term used to describe bonsai display.

SEKIJOJU Root over rock.

SEKKAI IOU GOUZAI Lime sulfur mix; substance used for preserving deadwood.

SEKKAN Internodes. Distance between nodes.

SENSEKI The search for stones.

SHAKAN Slanting style.

SHARI A length of deadwood appearing along the trunk.

SHARIMIKI Driftwood.

SHIDARE ZUKURI Weeping.

SHIN SHO New growth.

SHO HAKU Coniferous trees.

SHOHIN Bonsai up to 20 cm in height.

SHUKAN Main trunk in a grouping, clump, or raft style arrangement.

SOKAN Twin trunk.

SUIBAN Shallow water tray without drainage holes for displaying suiseki.

SUISEKI Viewing stones.

SUMI Japanese black ink.

TACHIAGARI Trunk region; base of the trunk at the ground line.

TAMA HI Round fertilizer (fertilizer cakes).

TAN SHI Short branch.

TANA WARI Separation of branch layers.

TANUKI Cheating style where sapling is attached to deadwood; also known as a Phoenix graft.

TATEKAE Reshaping trunk or branches.

TOKONOMA Traditional Japanese display area.

TORI KI MONO Bonsai obtained through air layering.

TORIKI Layering and dividing.

TSUGIKI Grafting.

UWA TSUCHI Surface soil.

WAKA GI Young tree (promising as bonsai material).

YAKU EDA Essential branch selection.

YAMA DORI MONO Bonsai obtained from collecting in the wild.

YATSUBUSA A variety exhibiting dwarfed characteristics.

YOBI TSUGI Approach graft.

YOSE UE Group planting.

ZOU KI A deciduous, fruit-bearing tree.